Intimate Marriage

Also by Barry and Emily McCarthy available from Carroll & Graf:

COUPLE SEXUAL AWARENESS
FEMALE SEXUAL AWARENESS
MALE SEXUAL AWARENESS by Barry McCarthy
SEXUAL AWARENESS

INTIMATE MARRIAGE

Developing a Life Partnership

Barry and Emily McCarthy

Carroll & Graf Publishers, Inc.
New York

First Carroll & Graf edition 1992

Carroll & Graf Publishers, Inc.
260 Fifth Avenue
New York, NY 10001

ISBN: 0-88184-824-7

Manufactured in the United States of America

Contents

ONE

Self-Esteem

Is marriage good for you? Does marriage promote personal satisfaction or does it trap you in a life which stifles individuality and independence? Are there happily married couples or does everyone compromise and settle for security because they fear divorce and being alone? With lessened cultural and religious stigma against divorce why do people stay married? Is marriage for women to obtain security and children? Is marriage for men to have regular sex and someone to take care of them, the house, and children, so they can pursue careers? Is it worth taking the risk to marry, when if it fails, divorce is so painful, bitter, and costly?

The relationship between self-esteem and marriage is complex. We will present guidelines, case studies, personal examples, and exercises that promote self-esteem and an intimate marriage. Whether married (happily or unhappily), single, divorced, or separated, it is crucial to increase awareness so you make choices which are in your best interest. Pundits comment that married people come to psychotherapy complaining of the frustrations and disappointment of marriage, saying how much better life would be if they were single. Single or divorced clients come to therapy saying the only thing that could make them happy and secure is to be married.

This is not a ''chicken or egg'' problem. A sense of self-worth is the cornerstone of psychological well-being. A satisfying and stable marriage is the best way to meet needs for intimacy and security. However, even the best marriage does not account for more than one-third of a person's self-esteem. Self-esteem is more important than marriage—we want to make this point clearly and unequivocally. Women and men who claim they need to be married or they will lose all their identity are fooling themselves. In some circumstances, such as a destructive or abusive marriage, the crucial step in rebuilding self-worth is to leave the marriage.

Theoretically, clinically, and personally, our stance is pro-marriage. There are no perfect people nor are there perfect marriages. All marriages go through difficult periods. Don't give up on a marriage because of disappointment, anger, or complex problems. Marriages where difficult issues are successfully dealt with not only survive, but are stronger for having confronted them. Marriages can be resilient. However, there are marriages that are fatally flawed. The marital bond of respect, trust, and intimacy either never existed or has been irreparably damaged. Rather than the marriage being based on positive influence, it is controlled by fear, destruction, and even terrorist tactics. Frighteningly, forty percent of murders of women are committed by spouses, ex-spouses, or lovers. Spouse abuse, often associated with alcohol or drug abuse, is shockingly prevalent. These marriages are not worth saving unless there is a dramatic turnaround.

We are respectful of marriage and the importance of taking seriously one's marital commitment. Nevertheless, a marriage that is destructive to one or both people is not worth preserving. According to the Alcoholics Anonymous program, which is very supportive of marriage and the family, if the marriage threatens the recovering alcoholic's sobriety, he must leave it. Neither is a destructive marriage to be preserved for the sake of religion, society, or finances. It is not in the best interest of children to see their parents fighting, being hateful, addicted, depressed, or intimidated. Staying together for "the sake of the children" is harmful to both children and adults.

RECIPROCAL RELATIONSHIP BETWEEN SELF-ESTEEM AND MARRIAGE

The model we propose emphasizes self-esteem that is promoted and reinforced by an intimate, stable marriage. Being in an intimate marriage brings out the best in you as a person. In loving your spouse, you respect the person you are because you are married to her. This doesn't happen because of fear of abandonment, or to win her approval. It occurs because you value who you are in this marriage and cherish your marital bond. One of the most satisfying aspects of marriage is sharing emotional and sexual intimacy.

Disclosing thoughts, feelings, perceptions, hopes and dreams, fears and worries—and being accepted for who you are promotes self-esteem. Your spouse respects and loves you not just for your strengths, but understands, accepts, and loves you with your weaknesses and problematic characteristics. Self-esteem is *not* a public relations "image." Self-esteem represents an integrated, clear view of yourself with good and bad characteristics, competence and achievements as well as failings and losses, feelings of joy and sadness, hopes and fears, acceptance of the past and plans for the future.

Marriage can be a hopeful, vital, and central component of self-esteem. Yet, self-esteem cannot be based solely, or even primarily, on marriage. No life component should contribute more than one-third to self-esteem. People look to marriage to bestow self-esteem; that is not its role. Self-esteem comes primarily from the individual. Marriage can nurture and enhance self-esteem, but cannot create it. An unhappy marriage destroys self-esteem.

WHO WE ARE AND WHY WE WROTE THIS BOOK

Barry and Emily McCarthy have been married twenty-five years. Barry is a practicing clinical psychologist and marriage therapist and Emily has a background in speech communication. We believe in these guidelines and try to apply them to our lives and marriage. We do not present ourselves as models nor do we have a perfect marriage. Each of us has strengths and weaknesses. Our marital bond of respect, trust, and intimacy has grown stronger over the years, but we do not take it for granted. We value each other and our marriage. Our goal is to make the next twenty-five years even more satisfying than the first twenty-five.

This is the fifth book we've collaborated on. Our previous books focused on sexual issues. Sexual self-esteem does not operate independently of personal self-esteem. Sexuality is a healthy, integral part of marriage, but not the most important part. We set out on this project to examine the relationship between self-esteem and marriage. Writing this book has improved our marriage. We hope reading it will serve the same function for you.

THE PRIMACY OF SELF-ESTEEM

People would be wise to wait until twenty-one, at the earliest, to marry. Marriage is best viewed as a well-thought-out commitment to share your life emotionally, financially, and sexually. Before you choose a spouse, you need to have a sense of who you are and what you value.

The person who marries because of an unplanned pregnancy, to get away from home, to feel loved, to rescue herself from depression or loneliness, as a way to escape fears of homosexuality, or because a best friend got married, is unlikely to choose well. Establish self-esteem and develop a life plan, including education or job training, before you marry. Marriage is a major life commitment and should not be entered into unless each person believes they can create an intimate, secure bond. Marriage is not a step to be taken lightly. People often marry for the wrong reasons, one of which is to boost self-esteem. Good marriages promote self-worth, but developing it is an individual responsibility, not the role of the spouse. Two case vignettes will more clearly make this point.

Donna. When Donna married at nineteen she told herself it was for all the right reasons and that she would have a perfect marriage. Her parents had divorced when she was eight, her mother remarried when Donna was twelve, and that marriage ended after three years. Her mother had given up on marriage for herself, but not for Donna. Like many children of divorce, Donna felt a need to prove she could establish a successful marriage.

She fell into the trap of idealizing her partner and marrying too young. Bruce was four years older (twenty-three), a nice guy, but immature and undirected. Two weeks before meeting Donna, a two-year relationship he had been in had ended, and he felt very unsettled. The woman had broken the engagement because she felt Bruce was unreliable. Donna was convinced she could help him. Bruce's friends and family loved Donna and believed marriage would settle him down. Donna was sure that with her love and support Bruce would be an ideal husband. She didn't view this marriage as a rescue operation, but, in retrospect, that's what it was.

Romantic love and naïve optimism didn't even last until the marriage. About three weeks before, Donna and Bruce had a disagreement, which turned into a screaming match, about the kind of flowers to have at church. He stormed out and disappeared for two days. She was very shaken. She had never seen him out of control and could not respect someone who reacted in that manner. Unfortunately, she let her mother and friends convince her that premarital jitters had caused the incident.

Only weeks after the wedding, Donna knew she had made a mistake. This was not a marriage but an arrangement. Though Bruce pretended to be a husband, he was less involved and responsible than a boyfriend. Donna had the tasks of cleaning, cooking, and looking out for him. Bruce said she had unrealistic romantic expectations, and that she should take what he offered. As the weeks turned to months, Donna became miserable. She was turning into an angry whiner. When self-esteem slides downward *with* marriage it indicates something dramatically awry. Donna's unhappiness and complaints were ignored or ridiculed by Bruce.

Donna thought extramarital affairs occurred only after several years of marriage and were caused by boredom and routine. In reality, extramarital affairs occur most frequently during the first three years of marriage. Bruce had his first affair two weeks after the ceremony, and had affairs throughout their brief time together. Donna felt it was her role to try to keep the marriage alive, but one person cannot carry a marriage.

As her self-esteem continued to decrease, she was desperate to find something to affirm her. Donna worked, kept contact with friends, and was active in sports and community groups. Although these activities were helpful, they did not offset the damage to her self-esteem. A man finding her attractive and flirting had a very powerful effect on her. In fact, too powerful—too much of a young woman's identity is dependent on the interest and approval of a man. That's why a spouse's rejection means so much. Donna was vulnerable but did not want to follow Bruce's example and have an affair. After talking to a recently divorced friend, she consulted an attorney who advised her to separate formally before beginning to date.

When Donna told Bruce she wanted a separation, she expected him to be relieved and to agree readily. Instead, he was tearful and begged her to stay. He said the fact that the marriage was not working was altogether his fault, and vowed to make any change she wanted. Donna was confused, and vacillated. They had a three-day second honeymoon and she hoped the marriage would turn around, but two weeks later Bruce reverted to his previous pattern of going out with the guys and lying about what he was doing. Donna suspected he had restarted an affair. She realized that Bruce was a dependent person; when faced with abandonment he reacted by making promises, but was not mature enough to keep them. Once respect is lost, it is difficult to revitalize the marital bond. Donna no longer respected Bruce and had no desire to remain married. With a sense of sadness, but this time with a firm resolve, she moved out and filed for divorce.

As a single-again woman, Donna had to reorganize her life and rebuild self-confidence. She enjoyed dating and found it validating to be with someone who found her attractive, but understood that a new relationship should not be the major element in regaining equilibrium. Donna had to reestablish friendships, reconnect to her family (who supported the decision to divorce), set up her apartment, reorganize finances, deal with the legal and psychological process of divorce, make career plans, and, most important, establish self-esteem as a single-again woman. She viewed the divorce as a learning process, not personal failure.

Donna planned to remarry. She had learned from this marriage and vowed to choose better the second time. Her choice would come from self-acceptance and awareness, not from a desperate need for a man to validate her or as a means of proving something to herself or anyone else. She would choose a mature partner she could respect and trust, and with whom she could share an emotionally and sexually intimate life.

Don. Don loved telling stories about how great it was to be single. At friends' weddings he'd make jokes about "another good man has been caught." His best friend's girlfriend disliked Don because of his wise-guy anti-marriage banter. Underneath the bravado, Don had the same needs for intimacy and security all men and women have.

The most charitable way to describe Don's parents' marriage would be to call it mediocre. Don remembers thinking from an early age that he did not want to live like that. For him, the secret to happiness was education. From fourth grade on, he was an all A student who was also active after school. At home, he stayed in his room doing homework and was an avid reader of science fiction. During high school, he formed special relationships with both his math and physics teachers, spending more time with their families than his own. At the state university, he was a charter member of the science club, and majored in engineering. Even as a freshman, when many students felt homesick and found academic demands daunting, Don loved college.

He pledged an engineering fraternity second semester freshman year. There are few female engineering majors (and a decade ago there were even fewer), so Don had little chance to develop social skills with women. One of his fraternity brothers fixed him up with a nursing student whom Don dated throughout college. Senior year, as many of his fraternity brothers became engaged, it was assumed Don, too, would marry his girlfriend of three years. Don understood that this was the socially desirable, expected thing, but was also aware that something critical was missing. He feared repeating the distant, cordial, but emotionally empty marriage of his parents. He would not allow himself to fall into that trap. It took courage to face the woman's hurt and anger and the disapproval of family and friends, but he broke off the relationship.

The remainder of senior year was lonely and emotionally painful, but Don did not regret his decision. He continued to put time and energy into the engineering program and job hunting. He got a lot of satisfaction from work, and this would remain a lifetime pattern—Don enjoyed engineering and professional accomplishments. At the same time, he knew that there needed to be a healthier balance in his life. He did value people.

Don talked about his feelings with his best friend's girlfriend, who had been angry with him after he broke up the three-year relationship. This young woman was planning to be married in a year, and conveyed a view of intimacy and marriage that opened a new world for Don. He and his friend went to work in the same city and the three of them remained close. Don was the best man at their wedding (he refrained from anti-marriage jokes). With the couple's encouragement, he began dating, this time trying to choose better, looking for an intimate relationship rather than a convenient arrangement. Don dated three women over the next year and a half. He didn't like the hurt feelings that came with the ending of a relationship, but had to admit he'd learned more about himself, women, and the process of relationships than he had during college.

A year later, Don fell in love with the most sexually attractive woman he'd ever dated. He was sure this would be permanent. His friend's wife sat down with him one afternoon and had a candid talk. Although she liked the new woman, she didn't believe they'd be a good match. Don was a serious, goal-oriented person who cared about succeeding at what he did, including marriage and a family. The woman had dropped out of college, had no plans or goals, loved fun and partying, and was not serious about life commitments. The friend asked Don whether he could imagine being happily married five years from now to this woman and see her as the mother of his children. The woman was good for Don in that she'd helped him relax and feel more confident about sex, but that's different from sharing a life together. Don was saddened to have his romantic fantasy burst, but realized that his friend was right. This relationship was difficult to end, continued much longer than it should have, but finally was over.

At twenty-six, Don felt ready to make a serious commitment. He had a better sense of himself and what he valued and wanted. He met Becky through mutual friends. Their first date was not romantic; it involved helping a friend move. Afterward, they went out for beer and pizza. Don and Becky were together informally four times before having their first formal date, a dinner dance to which Becky invited Don. Becky was a great dancer, but Don felt awkward and unsure of himself on the dance floor. Instead of trying to cover up the problem, he told her his concerns. Becky suggested he come to her house to practice. Don appreciated her not disparaging him or pretending it didn't matter. They kicked off their shoes—so it didn't hurt so much when Don stepped on her feet—and had a good time learning. Don came to enjoy dancing and being with Becky. Five months later, when Don told Becky he loved her, it was for real and for the right reasons.

DEVELOPING SELF-ESTEEM

You are not born with self-esteem. It develops from experience—from learning skills and becoming competent *socially, educationally, relationally, athletically*. Self-esteem is strongly influenced by external evaluations—grades, whether you were hired for a job, elected to an office, asked to the prom, rejected for club membership. Even more important are internal evaluations. Forty percent of self-esteem should come from external feedback, but sixty percent involves feelings of self-efficacy, comparing yourself with your goals and what you value. Unfortunately, for most people, external criteria are more important than internal perceptions and feelings. People compare themselves to an ideal, a TV star, the wealthiest person they know. The result—a sense of inadequacy. Compare yourself to your own realistic goals and desires. The worker who earns $100,000 but feels inadequate because someone in his office earns $115,000 will have low self-esteem. The person who sets a personal goal of earning $60,000 and gets a bonus so she earns $65,000, and is respected and liked by her coworkers, will have high self-esteem.

One key is setting personal goals and reaching them. Feeling good about yourself is important, but certainly not everything. The essence of self-esteem is respecting and accepting yourself for strengths and weaknesses, successes and failures, hopes and fears, stellar characteristics and unfortunate experiences. People with high self-esteem are congruent in their attitudes, behavior, and feelings. Their internal feelings of worth are reinforced by external feedback. Self-esteem is the central component in psychological well-being.

You are not an island, standing alone, apart from people. Relationships in which you feel cared for and respected are important. Close friendships in which you like, trust, and feel valued by others are crucial. One of the most, if not the most, important of relationships is an emotionally and sexually intimate one. For most people, this is fulfilled through marriage.

Self-esteem is promoted by an intimate, stable marriage. Married people report higher self-esteem than do single or divorced people. This is especially true for males, which contradicts the cultural myth of the happy bachelor.

Self-esteem comes before marital status. A person needn't be married to have it. The healthier his sense of himself, the more likely he is to choose a marital partner who will support and nurture him. Conversely, the less he values himself, the more likely he is to choose an inappropriate marital partner, and the difficult marriage will further lower self-esteem.

REALISTIC SELF-ESTEEM

Self-esteem is not a public relations scheme in which you pretend everything is perfect and make promises you cannot keep. Developing and maintaining realistic self-esteem means being aware of and accepting who you are, blemishes and all. Barry is one of the least mechanical men on the entire East Coast. Although he's not proud of that attribute, he has accepted it. Emily is a warm and likable person, but hates to entertain more than four people at a time. She dreads large, formal occasions (as does Barry). Although she wishes it could be otherwise, she accepts this limitation. We do not berate ourselves or each other for problematic characteristics.

If you feel self-respect only for positive attributes, your self-esteem will be unstable and you'll constantly feel vulnerable. What if my spouse discovers my faults—will I lose her respect and love? We are not suggesting you announce weaknesses and vulnerabilities to everyone. We do suggest you acknowledge weaknesses and incorporate these into realistic self-esteem. Problems and concerns should not be kept secret, but shared with close friends, especially your spouse.

Women tend to downplay their positive attributes. It's as

if acknowledging strengths is not feminine. Men are socialized to be competitive and goal-oriented. They have a difficult time disclosing weaknesses, vulnerabilities, and doubts. To do so would be unmasculine. The reality is that all human beings have strengths and weaknesses; there are no perfect people. Being respected and loved for the whole of you, not just good points, leads to a positive, stable self-esteem.

RELATIONSHIPS AND COMPETENCIES

Freud said that to be happy a person needs to "love and work." No element of life should contribute more than one-third to self-esteem. Pride in one's accomplishments and competencies is vital, and close friendships and parenting are very important, but each should not contribute more than one-third. Marriage, the major focus of this book, is another prime component, but even this should not be more than one-third. There needs to be a sense of balance, with multiple sources of self-esteem.

Relationships are not limited to marriage. They may include personal friends, couple friends, work friends, neighborhood friends, extended family, children, people with whom you share a hobby or sport. Especially important are close relationships where you can be open and vulnerable. That is why a marriage ending is such a devastating loss. It typically takes two years to heal afterward, and not just because of the loss of sex, love, financial stability, home or parental role. A special relationship in which you shared thoughts, feelings, and experiences has ended. Ex-spouses do not usually remain close friends. The more common outcome is anger, bitterness, and distrust. Your ex-spouse is often your worst critic. You need friendships and social support to deal with divorce.

SELF-ESTEEM AND DIVORCE

Divorce means a marriage, not a person, has failed; a divorced person can do no worse than view herself as a failure because of it. Our stance is pro-marriage. But divorce is not evil or an inherently bad outcome. Sometimes it is the healthiest choice and the most courageous action to take. Divorce is the *best* alternative to a marriage that is no longer viable or perhaps was fatally flawed from the beginning. Cultures that do not allow divorce or where it is heavily stigmatized are typified by mediocre marriages. The focus is on children, extended family, or same-sex social groups rather than on the quality of the marital bond. Marital stability is high, but marital satisfaction is low.

In large part because of the lessened stigma of divorce, the United States has one of the highest divorce rates in the world. It is also one of the few countries where wives are more likely than husbands to initiate a divorce. In other cultures, religion, the extended family, community pressure, and financial incentives serve to maintain mediocre or destructive marriages. In our culture, the marital bond has to be stronger and more vital because there are fewer external supports. This can promote better quality, healthier marriages. Divorce, for those marriages that end, may be a healthier outcome. If the individuals have learned about themselves and what is needed for an intimate, stable marriage, then a second marriage is likely to be successful. The United States has a very high remarriage rate. People may give up on one marriage, but not on the hope for a satisfying, secure marriage.

When Barry sees a couple who are unsure whether their marriage is worth preserving, his usual strategy is to propose a therapy contract to make a good faith six-month effort to revitalize the marital bond. The focus is on increasing respect, trust, and emotional and sexual intimacy. During the six-month period, there are no divorce threats and the couple are encouraged to assume that this marriage is worth saving. They attempt to reestablish a positive reciprocal relationship between self-esteem and the marital bond. For many couples this works, and there is a solid, renewed faith in themselves and their marriage. For most, confronting problems in their personal lives and marriage is a difficult, but worthwhile, process. Communication and problem solving are much improved. Although there are hurt feelings from the past, the couple is committed to a better quality marriage. They realize neither spouse is perfect, but that the marriage is of value and meets needs for intimacy and security.

Some couples find after six months that they feel better about themselves and the effort they've expended, but realize the marriage is not viable. When a marital bond has been broken, it's hard to put back together (the cracks are too apparent). Once respect and/or trust is lost, rebuilding it is an uphill struggle. Self-esteem is difficult to maintain when your spouse does not respect or trust you. Couples who have made the effort to salvage their marriage find it easier to separate in a nondestructive manner. They approach divorce feeling sad and regretful rather than angry, bitter, or vindictive. For couples who need a cooperative relationship to co-parent children, no matter what the custody arrangement, this is a real plus. Most important, it allows both people to leave the marriage without massive damage to self-esteem.

THE PLAN OF THIS BOOK

This book has two focuses. The first is self-esteem in marriage—how to develop, reinforce, and enhance it. The second focus is on the marital bond. We will explore how intimate, stable marriages are created and maintained. A satisfying marriage reinforces and strengthens each spouse's self-esteem, while a poor marriage undermines it.

Each chapter is self-contained; although connected to the major theme, it can stand by itself. Our suggestion would be to read Chapter Two, "Self-Esteem and Marriage," and other chapters from the first section that are relevant to you personally. The second section, Chapters Nine through Eleven, focuses on dealing with self-esteem and marital problems. Read chapters that are relevant to your situation and problem-solving focus. Couples, whether experiencing problems or not, would benefit from reading Chapter Twelve, "Revitalizing the Marital Bond."

This is a book of ideas and guidelines, not a do-it-yourself therapy book. Our assumption is that the more information and understanding individuals and couples have, the better their position to make decisions in their best interests. Knowledge is power. We draw on case studies of clients Barry has treated (their identities have been disguised), as well as personal experiences, to provide illustrations for concepts. There are exercises to help you assess and change attitudes, behaviors, and feelings. Do not feel pressured to engage in these. Do an exercise only if it seems relevant and would be helpful. The exercises provide a specific, personal approach to elements of your life and marriage.

Each person develops self-esteem, which is the core factor in psychological well-being. A satisfying, stable marriage nurtures and reinforces this core. Being in a respectful, trusting, and intimate marriage brings out the best in each person. Self-esteem and marriage should function in a positive, reciprocal manner. We hope this book's guidelines, exercises, and case examples will facilitate that process. If its effect is to make you aware of problems, we suggest seeking professional therapy in resolving them (Appendix I offers guidelines on finding an appropriate therapist). You deserve to have positive self-esteem, and a marriage that increases rather than subverts it. We hope this book increases awareness and understanding, and that implementing its concepts and guidelines will increase self-esteem and marital intimacy.

TWO

Self-Esteem and Marriage

Does marriage bestow self-esteem?

The romantic idea of a "perfect marriage" used to be, especially for women, the answer to any and all self-esteem problems. This made for great movies, love songs, and daytime talk shows, but for real people it set unrealistic and self-defeating expectations. There are no perfect people and no perfect marriages. If you use "perfect marriage" as your criterion for satisfaction you will feel inadequate, a second-class citizen.

Self-esteem is multifaceted, and needs to be understood in light of that complexity. No aspect of life, including marital status, should contribute more than one-third to your self-worth. Our model of self-esteem and marriage, which we try to practice in our own lives and marriage, emphasizes the spouse as your best and most trusted friend. Even then marriage cannot dominate self-esteem.

Psychological well-being is not dependent on being married. Our cultural view in the past held that women had to be married to be seen as successful. Single or divorced women were failures. People stayed in alienated or abusive marriages because of the stigma of divorce, an unrealistic and self-negating position.

The authors have a strong pro-marriage bias. A good (not "perfect") marriage meets needs for intimacy and security better than any other human relationship. For a marriage to be satisfying the essential components of the marital bond—respect, trust, and intimacy—must remain strong and vital. Stable marriages are based on a positive influence model, with both individuals and the marriage continuing to grow and change. Being married brings out the best in you as a person. There is reciprocity between self-esteem and marital satisfaction.

THE DECISION TO MARRY

Can people who are not married have self-esteem and a good life? Absolutely yes! Single, divorced, or widowed people with a sense of self-respect, competency in their job, a fulfilling personal life, and significant connections with others, experience higher levels of psychological well-being than those trapped in alienating, destructive, or abusive marriages. Finding someone to marry is not the solution to self-esteem problems. An unsatisfying marriage is a major factor in low self-esteem.

The decision of whether to marry and whom is one of the most crucial choices in life. Those who marry for the wrong reasons—to escape a poor family situation, or because of an unplanned pregnancy, or loneliness, or fear of never marrying, as a solution to another life problem, because friends are getting married, parental pressure, or romantic love—are likely to have a conflictual and disappointing marriage. We strongly encourage people to view, and plan, marriage as a choice and commitment. The right reasons to marry are an emotional *and* rational belief that your spouse is someone with whom respect, trust, and intimacy will grow. Marital choice should *not* be based on an idealized and romanticized view of the partner and the relationship. Marriage does not mean ownership of another person, it is a mutual commitment to share your lives.

Approach marital choice in a clear, aware manner, considering both emotional and rational factors in the decision-making. Disclose strengths and weaknesses so you reveal a realistic self-esteem rather than projecting an idealized image. In return, you need to have a clear view of your partner's strengths and weaknesses. Share hopes, plans, and dreams, but be clear that's not enough. Discuss hard issues such as where to live, career plans, contraception, sexuality, whether to have children, how to deal with families and in-laws, health or psychological problems, money issues, leisure activities and friendships, understandings concerning extramarital affairs, negative feelings, and problem-solving. A marital choice should be based on a realistic exchange of information, perceptions, feelings, and values, rather than romantic love. Emotional and sexual attraction is necessary for a viable marriage, but marital success requires much more. You have to create a joint life that meets each person's needs. Contrary to popular myth, love is *not* enough. Self-esteem and intimacy promote a healthy choice rather than a rescue operation based on romantic fantasy.

FEMALE-MALE DIFFERENCES

Is marriage more necessary or important for women? Does a woman need a man in order to feel she's a worthwhile person? Without a husband and children is a woman's life meaningless? Are men happier and more functional as bachelors? Is marriage a female trick to get men to be responsible for children? Are single men happier, healthier, and wealthier? These provocative questions make for great talk show and bar chatter, but are based on myths and misconceptions, not facts. The reality is that men are the ones who *need* marriage. Data show married men scoring higher on health and psychological measures than single or divorced men. Yet men value their marriages considerably less than women. What accounts for these confusing and paradoxical findings?

The socialization of women and men is quite different when it comes to marriage. Women emphasize relationships—friendships, extended family, work and community groups, children and caretaking—as integral to self-esteem. Men emphasize competition and achievement, and deemphasize relationships, including marriage. Women value intimacy considerably more than men. A marriage devoid of intimacy is viewed as unsatisfactory by the woman, but not necessarily so by the man. Males value sexuality, and complain if sex is lacking or infrequent. Females and males are socialized to be very different. The implicit assumption is that the male approach is the more functional one.

From our viewpoint, the male approach is problematic, since males need marriage more than females, although they value it less. Self-esteem has to come from a variety of sources, not primarily from career achievement, sports, and sex. Self-esteem is not a matter of competition, but of self-acceptance and integration. Self-esteem is integrally tied to relationships, especially marriage, parenting, and close friendships.

In truth, there are many more similarities than differences between women and men. Intellectually, emotionally, behaviorally, and sexually, women and men have much in common. Marriages work better when there is a recognition of similarities and mutual needs. Marriages based on equity in the distribution of power and sharing of roles result in greater satisfaction and stability. The female-male model of equity is applicable to a variety of relationships including friendships and work roles, but is especially important for the marital bond. Marriages that are respectful, trusting, intimate, and equitable are the most satisfying and secure.

SELF-ESTEEM AND MOTIVATION

It is difficult for an insecure person to have an equitable, intimate marriage. The woman who feels she is nothing without a man and the man dependent on a woman to take care of him are so controlled by deficit needs t sabotage a viable marital bond. Although this soun doxical, a crucial element in a successful marria awareness that you are a valuable person in your own right and will survive if not married. You need to have enough self-respect and confidence to maintain integrity if the partner or relationship becomes destructive. Self-help books as well as clinical textbooks are full of examples of people who cling to abusive and destructive relationships. The person remains married because of the belief that he has no worth without it.

Traditionally, because of the stigma of divorce, women were advised to stay with a husband, even if he was physically abusive, alcoholic, or abused the children. No marriage is worth that. Marriage is a choice, not a mandate. People who marry and stay married out of fear, guilt, or other negative motivation will have neither a satisfying marriage nor any sense of self-worth.

We advocate marriages that are intimate and stable. Marriage based on a positive influence model brings out the best in each spouse, building and nurturing self-esteem. A marriage that undercuts or destroys is not worth preserving, and to stay in it negates self-respect.

Self-esteem and marriage are best understood as reciprocal. Although marriage is a major contributor, it cannot be the only or dominating factor in self-esteem. Parenting, career, close friendships, extended family, activities and hobbies, religious, political, ethnic, or personal belief systems all contribute as well. An intimate, stable marriage facilitates self-esteem and a destructive marriage lowers it.

INTIMACY AND SELF-ESTEEM

Intimacy, one of the most misused terms in describing human behavior, is an integral component of the marital bond. Sexual intimacy is important, but emotional intimacy is crucial. Ideally, emotional and sexual intimacy would be integrated for each person and their marital bond.

Emotional intimacy involves disclosing feelings, perceptions, and both positive and negative thoughts. It means sharing vulnerabilities and doubts as well as strengths and hopes. Intimacy includes active involvement in the process of being a couple rather than viewing marriage as a static, completed object. Each spouse needs self-esteem in order to enter into a truly intimate marriage. The higher his self-esteem, the more fully he can give of himself. Conversely, the person who feels insecure cannot be intimate. For that person, intimacy is a desperate attempt to use marriage to gain self-esteem, an attempt doomed to failure. Positive motivation promotes positive behavior, negative motivation seldom results in positive behavior. Intimacy cannot compensate for low self-esteem. It's a one-two punch, self-esteem preceding intimacy. Intimacy reinforces each spouse's self-esteem and self-esteem increases the ability to be intimate.

Sexual intimacy is separate, but related. Couples report feeling vulnerable, yet close, when nude and being sexual. When we speak of sexual intimacy we are not referring principally to orgasm-oriented sex, which is satisfying but straightforward and goal-oriented. Sexual intimacy involves being open to giving and receiving nondemand pleasuring, sharing feelings, making sexual requests, being aroused and orgasmic, and engaging in afterplay. Sexual intimacy integrates emotional and sexual expression and is a bonding experience.

For young men, sex is automatic and autonomous; they need little from their partner. If sexuality is to remain vital and satisfying with aging, sexual expression needs to become more intimate and interactive. This is not a sign of weakening male potency, but an awareness that intimate, pleasure-oriented, give-and-take sexuality is satisfying for both the man and the woman. Rather than continuing to play out the rigid roles that couples learn from premarital experiences, sexual expression becomes more cooperative and flexible. Sex is more than genitals, intercourse, and orgasm. Sexuality is best when each spouse can initiate, say no, suggest alternative scenarios, engage in a variety of pleasuring techniques, and value emotional and sexual expression. This broad-based approach provides a solid basis for satisfying sexuality into your forties, fifties, sixties, seventies, and eighties.

THE ROLE OF MARRIAGE IN PROMOTING SELF-ESTEEM

Although self-esteem cannot be dependent on marriage, an intimate, stable marriage promotes it. In the traditional model of "for better or worse," marriage meant an *unconditional* acceptance of the spouse. This was enforced more rigidly for women; they were to accept their husbands and not complain. They discussed any problems with their mothers, mothers-in-law, or female friends. As the problematic marriage continued, disappointment and frustration grew. There was greater emotional distance and, in many marriages, alienation. Unconditional acceptance of a spouse is an unrealistic and unworkable model.

We advocate an aware and respectful acceptance as the basis for an intimate marriage. Instead of romantic idealization, you are aware of your spouse's strengths and weaknesses and are still loving. True acceptance is based on awareness of vulnerabilities and difficult characteristics, not just positive and attractive features. This would make an uninteresting film, but makes for a realistic, satisfying, and stable marriage.

Self-esteem is based on positive, realistic self-acceptance. Marriage facilitates self-esteem because your spouse is aware of who you are as a person, your sterling qualities as well as your faults, and continues to love and respect you. It is not unconditional: if you hurt your spouse, are destructive or disrespectful, or abuse your children, your behavior will not be tolerated and you will be confronted. Love does *not* mean "never having to say you're sorry." Marriage is based on a positive influence process that facilitates your being the person who is lovable and deserves to be respected.

Karen and Kevin. This couple are an excellent illustration of the positive, reciprocal relationship between self-esteem and marriage. Karen is forty-two and Kevin forty-three. They've been married seventeen years and have a fourteen-year-old daughter and a twelve-year-old son.

Karen grew up in a family and subculture that did not facilitate women's self-esteem. Her mother was viewed as a second-class citizen. Although she worked full time, she was underpaid, under-appreciated, and in addition to her job had to bear the entire burden of the house and children. Karen respected and loved her mother, but was committed to leading her life in a very different manner. In the section of Brooklyn where she grew up the rules for appropriate behavior for women and men were dramatically different. For Karen, as many women of her generation, the way to a new life was through education. As an adolescent, much of her self-esteem was tied to being the good student planning for college. Her mother strongly encouraged this goal.

When the time came for her to leave for college, Karen was reluctant and ambivalent. Several of her friends married that summer, and her boyfriend was urging her to remain in Brooklyn. If she wanted to go to college, she could attend the local community college. Karen mustered the courage to make the break and went three hundred miles away to the state university. She feels this was one of the most important and healthiest decisions of her life.

Her father and friends feared Karen would be an "old maid," that the best men were being taken. As Karen began to view the world through the eyes of a college student, it became clearer to her that she wanted a very different marriage from the one she had grown up with and those her high school friends were making. Karen could support herself as a computer analyst; marriage would mean giving up the freedom she valued, making plans, for example, without having to get anyone's permission. She enjoyed dating and having a boyfriend, but was not ready to settle into marriage. She needed to define who she was and what she valued before committing herself to sharing life with a man.

Karen's senior year at college was the most stressful since senior year in high school. Everyone seemed to know what was best for her. Her parents wanted her to return home, work, meet someone, and get married. Her best friend wanted Karen to go to graduate school with her. Her boyfriend wanted Karen to come with him to law school. Her zany friend wanted her to have a sophisticated life working for the airlines. Karen listened, but none of these options were in her best interest. With the help of a professor, she obtained a management training position in state government. This two-year on-the-job training program was excellent. She improved her understanding of computer systems and at the same time learned management skills that made her highly marketable. At the end of the two years, she was offered a state civil service position, but decided to accept a better job with more opportunities for advancement with a computer services firm.

Karen was comfortable taking responsibility for herself and her life. As her self-confidence and self-esteem grew, she felt open to marriage. At twenty-five, she felt aware and better prepared to choose an intimate partner. She was dating someone when a friend introduced her to Kevin. From their first meeting, Karen was aware that Kevin was a special person. Being friends for three months was a particularly good way to get to know him. They shared a number of interests including dancing, concern with social action issues, a willingness to volunteer time to help others, and a passion for boating and fishing. Most of their time was spent with other people, although they got into the habit of having breakfast together Sunday mornings. One Sunday Kevin surprised Karen by asking how serious she was about her present boyfriend. Karen started to make a joke, but caught herself and said she liked the fellow, but it was not a special relationship. She felt ready to establish an intimate relationship, but not with that man. Kevin took the opportunity to disclose his feelings, plans, and hopes.

Kevin had grown up in a very family-oriented environment. There were always aunts, uncles, and cousins around. No one in his family had been divorced, which Kevin saw as a positive. However, alcoholism was a problem that plagued many family members including his father. Kevin loved his father, but did not respect him. His parents colluded in denying the alcoholism. As his father lost job after job, the blame was put on politics and foreign companies rather than on the reality that the quality of his work had declined and that he missed more and more time because of his drinking. Additionally, Kevin's older brother was arrested for driving while intoxicated, which made Kevin even more determined not to follow that pattern in his life. If he was driving he had only one drink, and even if when not driving he was a moderate social drinker. Kevin was neither embarrassed nor apologetic about his family, but integral to his self-esteem was a commitment to live his life in a different manner, especially not to abuse alcohol.

Like Karen, Kevin valued education, and with a master's degree in public administration was the best-educated person in his family. He put a lot of time and energy into his career, and was committed to improving access to health care for minorities and the poor. Kevin had a number of friends and dated a good deal, although he'd had fewer serious relationships than Karen. He took the risk and told Karen he was very attracted to her.

Karen was flattered and not completely surprised. However, she wanted no part of a secret affair. She had seen too many friends caught in triangle relationships. She wasn't sure how attracted she was to Kevin. She was afraid that if dating didn't work, a good friendship would be lost. Karen promised Kevin she would think seriously about what he'd said. During the week, she asked a couple who knew him well what they thought. They encouraged Karen to pursue the relationship. The woman said that, of the men she knew, Kevin was the nicest and most trustworthy. Friday night

Karen ended her five-month relationship. She trie
in a nice way, but was firm in her decision. She
date Kevin unencumbered by concerns about anot

Romantic love is a special experience, not to be missed. Karen and Kevin look back on their first four months with fond memories. Talking on the phone until two in the morning, making love at noon, camping weekends and being sexual under the stars, dreaming of life together where everything would be bliss, waking at four in the morning to be sexual, and then going out for doughnuts, are special experiences and provide scintillating memories.

As they considered marriage, Kevin and Karen addressed the hard issues of being a couple—how and where they would live, agreements about money, time, careers, and friends, how to deal with each other's families, how to confront personal and couple problems. Romantic love is an energizer; it allows you to take the risk to be intimately involved. However, romantic love and the accompanying passion is short-lived. It seldom lasts a year and usually has decreased or disappeared by the time of marriage. Romantic love is not a good basis for marital choice nor does it help sustain the marital bond.

Karen and Kevin began developing a mature, stable intimacy. They discussed what their lives, as individuals and a couple, would be like five years into the future. Karen's respect and caring grew as she came to know Kevin more deeply. She appreciated his personal strength, life values, and interest in being an involved father. Karen was aware of his weaknesses—especially his tendencies to avoid emotional confrontation and to spend too much time watching sports on TV. Kevin found Karen's enthusiasm and openness to new people and experiences particularly attractive. He was impressed by her discipline and ability to see a project through to a successful conclusion. He was distressed by her moodiness, how easily she cried, her overconcern about money matters. She couldn't just buy something, but had to check five stores to make sure she got the best price. As they grew as a couple, they were able to address concerns and make changes, but each had to realize the other would never be ideal in the sensitive areas. Kevin would never be totally comfortable with emotional confrontation and Karen did not develop an easy manner about money. You love a spouse for their strengths and weaknesses. No person or marriage is perfect (that's for romantic novels).

Kevin and Karen nurtured their bond of respect, trust, and intimacy throughout the marriage. Sometimes that was easier than other times. All marriages have periods of stress, difficulty, and crisis. Many of these can be avoided, some cannot. Perhaps the major test of a marriage is its ability to cope with and survive difficult and painful experiences. Any couple can do well when external circumstances are favorable; the challenge is to work together and cope with a crisis or loss. Karen and Kevin remember their son's illness and four-month hospitalization as the most stressful time in the marriage. Their working together as a team—including crying and sharing fears that he could die—is recalled as one of their strongest, but most painful, moments. They would never want to go through it again, but take pride in the fact they survived (as did their son).

Marriage as a positive influence process has not been just a slogan for Karen and Kevin. They tried to maintain the balance between self-acceptance and spouse-acceptance with awareness of and ability to confront problem areas. They continue to make requests for change and to support each other in implementing a change plan. Kevin especially has had to monitor his tendency to let a problem fester until he became frustrated and disparaged Karen. Karen has had to monitor her tendency to nag. When the spouse becomes your worst critic, the marriage is in trouble. Rather than a positive influence, the marriage turns into a destructive power struggle.

Dealing with difficult issues is part of marriage. You need to be able to set reasonable limits and confront the spouse when he is not keeping agreements. This process improved self-esteem and has strengthened Kevin and Karen's marital bond. They have continued to grow as individuals and as a couple. Kevin realizes that he could not have become the person and father he is without the support and confrontation Karen has provided. Karen realizes that no husband is perfect, but without Kevin she would not have taken the career risks she has. She very much enjoys their marriage and family.

SELF-ESTEEM AND MARRIAGE

Ideally, a marriage serves to strengthen each person's self-esteem and the couple value their marital bond. Violent, abusive, or destructive marriages need not be tolerated. A marriage that assaults the person's self-esteem or is destructive to well-being does not deserve to be preserved.

We encourage couples to make a good-faith effort to address problem areas. In Barry's clinical work he has been impressed by some individuals' and couples' ability to deal with problem behaviors and make significant changes. Dramatic 360-degree changes are the rare exception. More common are gradual, but significant, incremental changes. These improve self-esteem and strengthen the view of the spouse as someone you trust, who has your best interest in mind, is responsive to you, and is capable of change.

As a personal example, Barry has always had difficulty with formal occasions. He hates wearing a suit and tie and feels terribly awkward where formal etiquette is observed. Emily was helpful in increasing his awareness of appropriate behavior and showed him how to match a suit, shirt, and tie. He doesn't enjoy these occasions, but does handle himself better. Emily had traveled little before meeting Barry, and found long plane rides and foreign cultures intimidating. She will never become a travel agent nor travel in a carefree manner throughout the world, but she does recall with pleasure their overseas trips.

CLOSING THOUGHTS

Whether twenty-five, fifty-five, or seventy-five, both people need to be open to change and the spouse's influence. Self-esteem has many sources and marriage should never be more than one-third of it. People who invest their entire identity in being married put intolerable pressure on the marriage. On the other end of the continuum, people who neglect their marriage and do not value the marital bond subvert the marriage as well as the spouse's self-esteem.

Marriage meets needs for intimacy and security better than any other human relationship. It enhances and reinforces self-esteem. Marriage cannot rest on its laurels—it needs to remain a vital bond that depends on a positive influence process to build self-esteem and enhance the intimate relationship.

from Heather Makgill

- share responsibilities home/kids
- good w/ children
- Ambitious
- respects my independence/me & career
- talk w/ share thoughts soulmate/ bestfriend
- enjoy life to fullest
- takes care of me

THREE

Choosing An Intimate Partner

Among life's crucial choices are whether to marry and to whom. Marriage is one of the most popular institutions in our culture; over ninety percent of people get married at least once. With a decision as important and complex, involving a multitude of rational and emotional factors, one would expect access to a plethora of courses, scientific studies, and thoughtful books and articles. Instead, Ann Landers and common-sense folklore predominate, reflecting a culture obsessed with romance. Falling in love is the number one reason people give for marrying. We look for someone to love us and make our lives complete.

We will present a psychological approach to marital choice, with guidelines applicable for a first marriage at twenty-five, a second marriage at thirty-five, or a widower remarrying at sixty-five. You need to consider these concepts and guidelines in light of your values, feelings, and options. Our model is quite different from conventional wisdom. You have to decide whether it meets your needs and life circumstances. Spouse choice is not a rational, logical, scientific exercise; it involves integrating rational and emotional components in making a commitment to share your lives.

Marriages based primarily on romantic love and/or sexual

attraction are doomed to failure. On another extreme are couples who objectively have everything in their favor—similar educational and religious backgrounds, support of family and friends, common interests and values—but are not sexually attracted. Such a couple will have a difficult time establishing an intimate marriage because loving feelings and sexual attraction are crucial. The more common pattern is the couple who are strongly attracted and passionately in love, but incompatible—one is achievement-oriented, the other easygoing; one desperately wants three children, the other has no interest in children; one wants to live close to the family, the other is planning to work in another state. They naïvely hope romantic love will overcome these hurdles. The reality is "love is *never* enough."

OUR MODEL OF SPOUSE CHOICE

Our model emphasizes three necessary components:

1. A shared view of life and marriage
2. Emotional and sexual attraction with the potential for intimacy
3. Discussion of hard issues and a five-year plan for each individual and their marital bond.

For a couple to have a reasonable chance of an intimate, stable marriage, all three components must be present. Couples who believe "as long as we love each other everything will be okay" are in for a rude awakening. Almost half of American marriages end in divorce, one of the highest in the world. Love and intimacy are essential but not sufficient, for a successful marriage. A shared view of life and marriage—including work, children, money, where to live, sex, friendships, extramarital sexuality, relationships with extended family, time together and time alone—are necessary ingredients for a satisfying, stable marriage.

We are opposed to the emphasis on romantic love because of its unrealistic expectations, idealization of the partner and relationship, and impossible promises such as “I'll think of another man,” and “I promise nothing bad will ever happen to you.” Romantic love usually lasts less than six months, seldom more than two years. If the marriage is to be happy and stable, initial attraction *must* develop into a mature, committed, broad-based emotional and sexual intimacy. The experience of a new love is entrancing and not to be missed. Feelings of attraction, desire, and passion provide special memories. However, romantic love is a poor basis for choosing a marital partner.

There is a negative correlation between being swept away by passion and choosing a spouse to share an intimate, stable marriage. We are not saying this because we are opposed to wild and crazy sex or intense emotional expression, but from empirical and clinical evidence. The “hot and crazy” romance is better for weeks or months than over a lifetime. Overwhelming feelings of love and passion are likely to turn to equally intense emotions of disappointment and anger. To state this positively: attraction, desire, and loving feelings are crucial in marital choice. However, overwhelming intensity, desperateness, and the feeling that your life has no worth unless the person reciprocates indicates that you are in an unhealthy relationship. Popular psychology books call this “love addiction.” Intensity and desperateness are *not* measures of true love.

On the other extreme are individuals who are great platonic friends but would find marriage frustrating and unhappy. Marriages without emotional intimacy and erotic attraction become a hollow shell. Marriage is primarily a respectful and trusting bond, but emotional and sexual attraction is crucial. Having similar beliefs, interests, and values is important but cannot compensate for a lack of intimacy and sexual connection. Platonic friendships seldom become successful marriages. The usual outcome is loss of a friend.

Many people find the concept of a five-year plan objectionable, feeling that it robs marriage of mystique and romance. This stance obscures the necessity of discussing the hard issues openly and in detail. Cutting away romantic idealism will enhance rather than damage an intimate relationship. If one spouse wants children and the other has a vasectomy, there's no room for a compromise. You need to reach understandings about communication and conflict resolution, the role of careers and money, children and parenting, sexual expression and extramarital affairs, where and how you'll live. These are not set in concrete—you change as individuals and your relationship changes, so there needs to be openness and flexibility. However, one spouse cannot unilaterally change an agreement, especially without saying anything. Old agreements need to be revised and new issues discussed so you remain aware of each other's feelings, values, hopes, and goals.

It is especially important not to hide a major secret such as a child from a previous marriage, a history of depression or sexual dysfunction, threat of bankruptcy, or shame over being physically or sexually abused as a child. A marriage built on a secret or false claims has an insecure foundation. You need to accept and respect yourself for who you are, enjoying successes and accepting, not denying, defeats and sad experiences. Initially, if you want to impress someone it's socially desirable to put your best foot forward. However, you need to be truthful when discussing a marital commitment. If she can't accept you for who you are, you would be better off not married to this woman. Respect and trust are based on knowledge.

You need an understanding of each other's personality and background, hopes and plans, view of life and marriage. Can attraction grow into mature sexuality and intimacy? Can you discuss attitudes, behavior, and feelings about a range of life issues? Are you willing to create and share a life together?

A PERSONAL NOTE

When we decided to marry we followed most aspects of this model, but made some decisions that did not coincide with scientific knowledge or these guidelines. Are we hypocrites? We think not. We believe in the importance of individual responsibility—ultimately it is the individual who must choose what is in his best interest. Scientific knowledge and guidelines have value and need to be carefully weighed, but no one can make life and marital decisions for you.

We fully and honestly disclosed difficult issues from our family of origin. We made agreements about what we wanted from our marriage and traps to be aware of. We knew we would have to work hard to have a successful marriage since we had poor marital models.

Guidelines based on empirical research and clinical experience are of value, but each person and couple have to decide whether these guidelines are relevant to their values and situation. One guideline we believe in clinically and which has been confirmed by empirical research is that the couple should be involved for a year before marrying. From our first date until our marriage day was exactly four months. We would not advise readers to do that, but have no regrets about our decision or how we made it. If you make a decision different from a guideline, get the necessary information, discuss it with a respected and trusted person. Be sure it is well thought out and has a good chance of success.

MARITAL GUIDELINES

Two strongly recommended guidelines are to wait at least until the age of twenty-one to marry, and to delay having a baby for two years. This allows you to develop and strengthen your marital bond before becoming a family. Human beings are complex and individualistic, so there will always be examples of couples who violate every guideline and overcome incredible odds to achieve a satisfying marriage. We have great admiration for them. Determination to succeed is extremely important in marriage. However, the couple will have to work harder. Over seventy-five percent of couples who marry before they are twenty-one will divorce. Those who beat the odds and have a successful marriage can take special pride, but we advise careful consideration and consultation before marrying due to a pregnancy or if the couple is under twenty-one.

Another example of high-risk marriages are biracial couples or those with large age differences. Couples with similar educational, religious, age and racial backgrounds have a greater chance for marital stability. A biracial couple has to work harder to achieve and maintain a successful marriage. They not only need to overcome societal prejudice, but increase awareness of each other's backgrounds, feelings, and attitudes. They need to build a support system, couple friends, and/or extended family for help through difficult times. Couples with large age differences have to deal with gossip and innuendo, especially when the woman is older than the man. More importantly, they need to bridge chasms in terms of attitudes and experiences so there is a sense of equity in the relationship. The process of increasing understanding and reaching agreements is complex and time-consuming, but is vital if the marriage is to thrive.

In choosing an intimate partner be aware of what you need and value. Share hopes, fears, feelings, concerns, and plan a life that will meet individual and couple needs. The first two years of marriage are the most important because they form a foundation—for better or worse—of your couple style. Marriages are not static. You need to continue to think, talk, and put energy into the relationship. The marital bond alters as individual and life circumstances change. A sign of a viable marriage is its ability to adapt and be resilient. Stagnation results in a frustrating and unsatisfactory marriage. Choose a spouse who can grow with you.

Marriages do not come with money-back guarantees. Even couples who follow all the guidelines and appear to be a perfect match need to put time and energy into developing a communication and problem-solving style. If they assume they are a special couple and take the marriage for granted, they will encounter major trouble. Even marriages that have thrived for twenty years cannot rest on their laurels. For a marriage to remain satisfying and secure it needs continued energy and attention.

Exercise: Who You Are and What You Want From Marriage

Before you choose a marital partner, be aware of your attitudes, values, and feelings, and what you need and want in a marriage. For example, if religion is important, marrying an atheist could result in serious problems. If you are ambitious, choosing a low-key person who does not want you to work hard will lead to conflict. If you are an athletic person who emphasizes keeping fit, you would have difficulty with a couch potato who smokes and drinks.

List five factors that are centrally important to you in life and marriage. Be as specific as possible. For example, I want to live in this area or overseas; I want a family-oriented life or I don't want children; I want to be financially successful or money is not a major factor; I want someone with a sense of humor who likes to have fun or I want a soulmate with whom to share my deepest feelings; I want someone who is responsible and will take care of me or I want an independent person who is comfortable with having her own life; communicating feelings is crucial or I only enjoy intellectual discussions; affection and sexuality are important or they play a minor role; I need to socialize with friends or I want to do things as a couple; someone shorter than I am is important or physical characteristics matter little; I like having weekly contact with extended family or I prefer seeing relatives only during holidays; I care passionately about music, politics, sports or the arts. These are not right-wrong choices, but your needs and desires. Once you are clear about what you value, it is easier to think about what you want and need from an intimate partner.

Partner choice is both emotional and rational. The rational components are easier to specify. The old argument of whether likes or dislikes attract has been empirically answered. People [illegible] iterests and values make better spouses. On incon- [illegible] ues such as one person preferring jazz to rap, [illegible] es, cats to dogs, formal to informal dinner parties, [illegible] rences can add spice and variety. However, one [illegible] ing children and extended family contact and the other desiring to remain childless so his is/she is free to change jobs and cities frequently, are core incompatibilities that romantic love will not sweep away.

VALUING AN INTIMATE MARRIAGE

A crucial dimension is how strongly the marriage is valued. For some, marriage is the bedrock of self-esteem, the most important factor in life. For others, marriage is socially desirable and not being married is a sign of personal inadequacy, but once married it is not a central life dimension. A pattern in many marriages is the "pursuer" and "avoider." Typically, it is the woman who seeks greater emotional involvement. The man says I love you and live with you so let me get on with my work, hobbies, and friends. Male socialization encourages a "minimal contact" marriage, but one that can be depended on. The woman complains to female friends and buys self-help books to understand men and increase intimacy. The self-esteem and marriage book market caters to women, which has the adverse effect of increasing unrealistic expectations and subsequent frustration. The woman assumes that it is her responsibility to make the marriage fulfilling and that she's a failure if it isn't. The male complains of excessive demands on him, is stressed by her emotional needs, and withdraws further, causing her to pursue more relentlessly. The "pursuer-avoider" pattern becomes more intense and frustrating. It serves to devalue the marriage, each spouse viewing the other as the "problem."

If you read marriage books, you would conclude that everyone supports the idea of intense marital intimacy. In reality, the crucial dimension is reaching a comfortable level of intimacy. There are satisfying marriages with a great deal of personal autonomy and moderate emotional intimacy. If that is satisfying, accept it rather than striving for the ''best friend'' marriage model we advocate. Some couples find too much intimacy intrusive and emotionally suffocating. Reach an understanding on a comfortable level and avoid the extremes of emotional isolation or a symbiotic relationship in which you believe you have no value without your spouse. The key is reaching a mutually acceptable level of marital intimacy.

The experience of falling in love and being sexually swept away is highly valued in our culture. However, romantic love is an unstable base for a marriage. Attraction needs to contain the potential for intimacy that will grow, not a chemical attraction that radiates powerfully but burns out and dies within two years. Therapists' offices are full of couples who report passion the first few months, but now look at the spouse and say, ''I don't even like this person.'' Don't make spouse choice dependent on emotional impulse or passion. How will you feel about your potential partner five years in the future? Will emotional and sexual intimacy grow? Is this someone you respect, trust, like? Can you share a life of good and bad experiences with him?

Lorna. When she was a girl, Lorna remembers, she asked her mother how she would know if she was in love. Her mother laughed and said, ''You'll know.'' Lorna's favorite movie was *Fiddler on the Roof*; she identified with the three daughters. She was convinced that choosing whom to marry was the most important decision of her life. Whom would she fall in love with?

Lorna was the youngest of three children. Her sister married at twenty to a man Lorna couldn't stand. Later, she learned that her sister's pregnancy was the reason for the marriage. Lorna loved being an aunt and helping with the baby, giving her ample opportunity to observe an unhappy marriage up close. She became committed to marrying later and not being pregnant at marriage. She wanted a husband who would be a soulmate, someone to share deeply with. Seeing the void in her sister's marriage made her value emotional intimacy.

Lorna's brother married at twenty-six (his wife was not pregnant). She liked her sister-in-law, but thought it was a strange match. Her brother was a gregarious guy who enjoyed social and sports activities. His wife was quiet, serious, and extremely involved with her family. She was anxious in situations involving crowds. Within a year she showed symptoms of agoraphobia, causing social problems that stressed the marriage. Although from childhood on Lorna had anticipated marriage, and felt it was the only path to happiness, seeing her siblings in difficult marriages put this in a different perspective. She realized that remaining single would be superior to being in a problematic marriage.

Lorna had an associate degree in medical technology and worked in a hospital. She enjoyed meeting men and dating. She did not like doctors, finding them arrogant and elitist, although several of her friends dreamed of marrying physicians. She resented the hierarchial organization of the hospital, but realized that to advance in medical technology she needed to complete her bachelor's degree.

Part-time evening study is a different educational and social experience from full-time college life. Night students comprise a wide range of backgrounds and ages. Lorna was asked out by a number of men. She found it fascinating to date an older, divorced man and relate to his children. Three years before, she would hardly have thought of dating this person, or of contemplating marriage to him. That relationship ended when Lorna became uncomfortable with how harsh he was with his children. She wanted children, and wanted to be married to a man who would be an involved, nurturing father.

At twenty-five, Lorna was clear about what she did *not* want in a partner and marriage. She no longer believed marriage was the most important factor in a woman's life, and felt that her single life was worthwhile and satisfying. She remained enthusiastic about marriage and children, but did not feel desperate. She'd seen many friends so anxious to marry that they pursued marginal or destructive relationships. Lorna want to marry, would be disappointed if she did not, but knew she could have a good life as a single woman.

Gene had been in two of Lorna's classes and they had chatted briefly. During a class break, Gene mentioned the problems his son was having with allergies—he was not pleased with the allergist the pediatrician had recommended. Lorna knew a competent pediatric allergist from her hospital contacts. She took Gene's phone number and told him she would get the information and leave it on his answering machine. Two weeks later Gene thanked her profusely for the referral and asked if he could buy her coffee and dessert after class. Lorna said yes, partly because she found this a refreshing invitation as opposed to the usual "Let's meet for a drink." She mentioned this and Gene took a deep breath and said he had been a member of Alcoholics Anonymous for the past three years. He was not embarrassed or guilty about his alcoholism, but usually didn't tell people immediately. He wanted them to get to know who he was before revealing his history of alcohol abuse and recovery.

As Lorna sat across the table she experienced two conflicting feelings. She felt attracted to thirty-two-year-old Gene, who was handsome and verbal. She felt strange about the age difference, his history of alcoholism, and his having a child. None of these factors were on the list of attributes she desired. Yet, this was the reality of Gene, and she remained open to the possibility of a relationship.

Lorna enjoyed getting to know Gene through real-life activities as well as formal dates. She was surprised by her enjoyment of his son's soccer games and their doing things as a threesome. She went to an A.A. meeting where Gene was the speaker and heard the full story of his alcoholism. As well as having fun, and sharing feelings and experiences, they discussed serious life issues. Lorna had a positive attitude toward touching and sexuality (including being a conscientious user of birth control pills). Developing a sexual relationship increased their level of intimacy. As a young woman, Lorna remembered thinking that if she was sexually aroused she must have loving feelings toward the man. After several relationships, she realized she could be sexually aroused even if the relationship was marginal, but felt best about sexuality when she was romantically attracted and emotionally intimate.

As their relationship grew, Lorna realized she was falling in love with Gene. She decided this would be a good time to check out the hard issues, and invited him to go to a one-day workshop and stay for the weekend. Lorna's core factors in choosing a marital partner were a man who would respect her and her career, who wanted children and would be an active father, would live in the area where she currently lived, and who wanted a best friend or soulmate marital relationship. Before asking about his perceptions and feelings, Lorna disclosed her hopes and plans so that Gene would know where she was coming from. When one partner is open and self-discloses, the other is more likely to do the same. Gene appreciated Lorna's openness and, in turn, shared his hopes, dreams, and concerns. He definitely wanted to remarry and have a second family. The hardest element for him was the soulmate concept. He'd learned to talk about feelings in his A.A. group, but self-disclosure and intimacy did not come easily. As the weekend went on they talked in depth about personal strengths and weaknesses, hopes and fears.

Two months later, Lorna and Gene decided to marry. During that two-month period they met each other's families, discussed what kind of life they envisioned in the next five years, and shared—rationally and emotionally—attitudes and values, personal and couple plans, hopes and anxieties. Lorna felt ready to enter into the complexity of a blended family. Both she and Gene were committed to making this a successful marriage, to share the problems as well as the joy and intimacy.

PARTNER CHOICE IN A SECOND MARRIAGE

Do forty-three-year-old divorced people choose better than never-married twenty-three-year-olds? Not necessarily. Hopefully, a second marriage will be more fulfilling than the first. That will happen if you honestly integrate what you learned about yourself and the process of an intimate relationship and utilize that learning in choosing a second spouse. Too often the same mistakes are repeated. The woman whose first husband was exceptionally good-looking but disappointed her by being irresponsible about money marries a good-looking second husband who disappoints her by wanting to do nothing but hang around the apartment and convince her to have five children. She hasn't identified what she wants in a husband and marriage. She knows what kind of man initially attracts her and hopes he'll know what will make her happy. Many women and men know what they don't want, but have not identified what they desire and need.

Second marriages can be more successful and lasting because of greater maturity and self-awareness. The necessity to make a better choice is greater because you have to deal with the complexity and challenges of blended families. A common problem is that your self-esteem may be lowered during divorce, so you meet a partner and rush into marriage as a way to rebuild it. Males are particularly vulnerable to this. The first year after divorce is the most common time to remarry; our suggestion is to rebuild self-esteem instead of looking for another person to do it for you. We caution against a rebound marriage, entered into when you are feeling so pained by the divorce that you are desperate to remarry and be taken care of, or you want to prove something to your ex-spouse or yourself. The suggested guideline is to wait at least two years after divorce before considering remarriage. Be sure marital choice is for the right reason, a commitment to share a life with this person. Talking out difficult issues and making a five-year plan are a necessity.

Leah-Ann and Robert. Leah-Ann wishes that when couples divorce, the ex-husband could just disappear. For her, the hardest part of being divorced was dealing with her ex-husband about their children. Leah-Ann was pregnant at the time of their marriage—she has a six-year-old son and a four-year-old daughter. The marriage ended six months after their daughter's birth. Her ex-husband and new wife see the children every other weekend and from two to four weeks during the summer. Friends wondered if Leah-Ann was jealous of her ex's new marriage. Leah-Ann could honestly say she was happy not being married to him and believed his second marriage would be problematic. In fact, the new wife had called her and Leah-Ann wisely chose not to become involved in giving information or emotional support. Leah-Ann tried to stay away from personal issues, and dealt with her ex-husband only about parenting.

When her mother asked if she planned to remarry, Leah-Ann said it would take a special man and a special relationship. What she liked best about being single were the variety of people, activities, and relationships in her life; she disliked the dating scene and sex games. She used the birth control pill conscientiously, even if she was not sexually active. She insisted that males use condoms to protect against sexually transmitted diseases and the HIV virus. Leah-Ann felt sexually aware and comfortable, but disliked feeling pressured, and bristled at being called inhibited or frigid when she said no. She found the sex game to be even worse than during adolescence; nevertheless, she preferred being single with all its hassles to being trapped in a loveless marriage.

Robert was also single again, but with a very difficult set of circumstances. His wife had died shortly after giving birth to their son. To further complicate this emotionally painful situation, Robert believed that her death was a result of hospital negligence. For two years he went through the confusing and frustrating labyrinth of medical malpractice litigation. The case was eventually settled for a large sum of money, but Robert did not experience the sense of vindication and psychological relief he'd hoped. Although relatives and friends were supportive, parenting his son was very difficult. Like many males, he had assumed that his wife would be the primary parent and felt unprepared to father a baby.

With the settlement money he bought a new house and could afford child care, but evenings after putting the boy to sleep were particularly lonely. He especially found difficult the absence of someone with whom to talk and share parenting concerns.

Robert did have opportunities to date. Several women were interested in marriage and excited about the idea of mothering his son. Robert felt he needed time to mourn the loss of his wife and didn't want to marry out of neediness. His father had remarried at sixty-eight, four months after Robert's mother died. Although Robert was not judgmental, he knew his father was afraid of being alone, and had remarried to have someone to keep him company and take care of him, a common pattern among widowers. Robert wanted to remarry, but needed to be sure he was doing it for the right reasons. He was aware of his tendency to idealize his first wife, and had no intention of falling into the "comparison trap." He wanted a second marriage that could stand on its own.

Robert and Leah-Ann met at a neighborhood playground. He was impressed by how she related to her children. The combination of attention, nurturance, and limit-setting was what he himself strove to achieve. Robert and Leah-Ann saw each other at the playground on weekends and chatted about children and parenting. She loaned him her two favorite books—one on parenting boys and the other on the challenges of being a single parent.

On Sundays after the playground, Leah-Ann took the children to a family restaurant (she tries to stay away from fast food places and advocates eating well and nutritionally). One Sunday she invited Robert and his son to join them. Robert's usual routine was to put the child down for a nap and watch sports on TV in the afternoon, but this was a much more pleasant alternative. After lunch, Leah-Ann suggested they go to her house where his son could take a nap. Robert had a range of feelings sitting in the kitchen, talking and drinking coffee. There was a sense of normalcy and family that he had envisioned when first married. There was also a strong sexual attraction and concern over "making a pass," which made him feel like an adolescent. Leah-Ann had similar feelings. Neither wanted to verbalize what was happening because each feared rejection and disrupting a comfortable friendship.

Afternoon turned to evening, and Robert volunteered to cook his special meat loaf. Cooking for five is different from cooking for two, and he and Leah-Ann enjoyed working together. Her children entertained his son. Although there was one big squabble, it was a pleasant evening. When they left, Leah-Ann kissed the boy and impulsively gave Robert a kiss. He thought about the kiss all night.

The next morning, he called and invited Leah-Ann to listen to his favorite jazz group the following Friday night. Leah-Ann thanked Robert for the invitation, but asked if she could think about it for a day and check on babysitters. In the three years she'd been divorced, she'd dated and had affairs, but hadn't involved these men with her children. The idea of dating someone who knew her children and whose son was a playmate seemed risky. It was not worth doing unless there was a possibility of a serious relationship. She reviewed what she knew of Robert and decided he was worth the risk. She called and said she was very interested in seeing him, but smoky nightclubs were not her favorite place and jazz was not her favorite music. Instead she invited him to her house for a late dinner after the kids were asleep.

Robert arrived with flowers and wine, and Leah-Ann was definitely feeling attracted and romantic, but rather than allowing herself to be swept away, she asked whether this was just for fun or might be something serious. Robert was not someone who used seduction "lines" or overpromised. He too realized that this could be a special relationship with higher stakes because of the children. He was very attracted to Leah-Ann, but couldn't make promises about love and marriage. He was open to an intimate relationship and promised to be truthful about feelings as the relationship progressed. They had a very late dinner after making love.

Second marriages are riskier and more difficult than first marriages for both emotional and practical reasons. It is important to discuss strengths and weaknesses so that you are aware of the emotional baggage and traps each person brings to this marriage. The couple needs to discuss hopes and plans as well as potential problems, especially involving the blended family. Leah-Ann and Robert did this throughout the eight months before they set a wedding date. Robert was the more romantic and optimistic one. He was committed to Leah-Ann and believed they could overcome any problems. His biggest hurdle was parental opposition to marrying a divorced woman with two children. Robert told his parents that at thirty-two he was responsible for his decisions. He appreciated their feedback and concern, but they needed to respect his judgment.

Leah-Ann felt loving, but had concerns about financial, parenting, and practical matters. She was used to managing her financial affairs and worried that Robert, reverting to the traditional male role, would want to take control. She insisted, and he agreed to shared money management. Having a younger child as an occasional playmate is one thing, but step-sibling relationships can be confusing and difficult. Leah-Ann was sensitive to her son's feelings about losing his special status in the family. To make this blended family work would require awareness, communication, and tolerance. It would take months and years, not hours and days. Leah-Ann was aware of religious, cultural, and financial differences. She encouraged Robert to talk about these hard issues and reach mutual understandings and agreements. The combination of Robert's optimism and Leah-Ann's realism have served them well throughout their marriage. Both are committed to having an intimate, durable marriage, and a successful blended family.

MARRIAGE AS A PROCESS

Much romantic and common-sense advice centers on falling in love with the right person. We believe in marrying for the right reasons and choosing a spouse based on disclosing strengths and weaknesses with a shared view of life and marriage. However, choice of partner is not the crucial factor in a successful marriage. Contrary to the romantic love myth, there is not one special person you have to find. You could be successfully married to one of a number of people. The crucial factor is motivation and commitment to develop and maintain a vital marital bond. There are some marriages that are fatally flawed—no amount of motivation or therapy can make a couple viable if they do not respect or trust each other or feel attraction and intimacy.

The major enemies of marriage are unrealistic expectations and benign neglect. The myth that love should be enough and that once married you will live happily ever after is poisonous and destructive. The reality is that a good marriage needs consistent time and energy. The person you marry at twenty-four will not stay the same at forty-four or sixty-four. This is why it is important to choose a person with whom you can share your life sexually, financially, emotionally, and practically. Respect, trust, and intimacy grow in a satisfying marriage.

Our favorite metaphor for marriage is a garden. It is important to choose a spot where the ground is good and there is access to sunlight and water. It's important to choose an intimate partner where there is a shared view of life with emotional and sexual attraction. A garden needs tending, watering, planting, and weeding. The first two years of a marriage are crucial to establish and strengthen the marital bond and in learning to live together. A garden needs consistent attention to thrive—crop rotation and addition of new plants, water, and cultivation. A garden, like a marriage, cannot rest on its laurels. All have problems—drought, insect infestation, plantings that don't take—problems that can't be denied or ignored and must be attended to and resolved if the garden is to thrive and mature. This is even truer of a marriage—

couples who resolve problems and deal with crises have stronger, more secure marital bonds. When we travel, we enjoy visiting old, well-kept gardens and admire how they've maintained their beauty. In healthy marriages, each spouse changes as does the marriage. The sense of pride in how their lives and marriage evolve increases self-esteem. Choosing an intimate partner is necessary, but not sufficient, for a satisfying, secure marriage. Marriage is an ongoing process; it requires continual time and psychological energy. It's well worth the effort because a good marriage meets intimacy and security needs better than any other relationship.

FOUR

The Marital Bond: Respect, Trust, and Intimacy

Respect, trust, and intimacy is our mantra for marriage—these are the core components for a satisfying and stable relationship. In traditional marital theory, the emphasis has been on love and communication. Although we value love and communication, they have been oversold as solving all marital problems. One of our favorite sayings is "love is never enough."

Romantic love gives you the courage to initiate and risk a new relationship, but unless romance grows into mature intimacy, it will subvert a marriage. Romantic love gives way to disillusion and anger; it works better in songs and movies than in the everyday life of a married couple. Emotional and sexual intimacy is much superior to romantic love in creating a satisfying, stable marriage.

Communication counts in marriage. There are significant differences in the communication patterns of satisfied and dissatisfied couples. Satisfied couples discuss personal issues and feelings, are empathic listeners, reveal thoughts and plans, seldom disparage each other, discuss alternatives and solve problems, and are emotionally affirmative and supportive. However, contrary to popular myth, communication is not enough. Couples believe that if they communicate more, everything will be okay. In truth, if there is disrespect, inequity in power, lack of trust, or a dearth of intimacy, all the communication techniques in the world will not help.

The marital bond is more than its component parts. We will examine each separately and suggest an exercise to increase awareness and enhance that component.

RESPECT

Self-respect and respect for the spouse are the cornerstones of an intimate marriage. Without self-respect you lose self-esteem. When you lose respect for your spouse, other aspects of the marriage begin to deteriorate. When Barry sees a couple who are distrustful, feel emotionally alienated, or who communicate in a destructive manner, he feels hopeful as long as the couple are motivated. However, when he sees a couple who are disdainful or disrespectful, he questions the viability of their marriage. The worst situation is one in which one person has low self-esteem, and the spouse takes pleasure in being his worst critic. How can you build self-respect? The most important ingredient is respecting how you handle your life and marriage. You cannot expect your spouse to respect you if you don't respect yourself.

Self-respect involves a realistic appraisal of who you are, with strengths and vulnerabilities. It includes more than the marriage; it's crucial to have a full and satisfying life apart from the spouse. This provides a sense of personal competency and allows you to view the marriage in perspective. The people most devastated by divorce are those who put their whole lives and self-esteem into the marriage in the mistaken belief that this is the way it should be. Successful marriages involve two people who value their individuality and self-esteem.

A crucial component is respecting how you relate to your spouse. The person who looks to the spouse for affirmation depends totally on the spouse to entertain him, or feels lonely or depressed if not without the spouse, or cannot develop a sense of himself as an independent, competent person. He views himself as incomplete without his spouse (the pop psychology term is "codependent"). You have to value yourself as an independent person if you are to genuinely respect your spouse and marital bond. When you respect yourself, it's easier for your spouse to respect you.

Exercise One: Respect

Do this exercise by yourself and then share it with your spouse. We suggest that you write this out to make it more concrete and personal. Divide the page into four columns. In the first column, focus on the characteristics and experiences that enhance self-respect. In the second column, write down the elements that cause you to respect yourself in the marriage; in the third, what you respect about your spouse; and lastly, what you respect about your marital bond. Try to keep these separate. Be as clear and specific as you can; don't write what sounds good or is socially desirable. Be truthful.

Under personal characteristics, think about the past as well as the present, minor elements as well as major. We suggest identifying at least five characteristics, although we've seen individuals who list twenty-five attributes. Examples include attaining an associate degree in office management, gaining a starting position on a community soccer team, remodeling a kitchen or bathroom, learning to change diapers instead of waiting for your spouse to do it, teaching your child to fish, receiving a merit pay award, driving an elderly neighbor to medical appointments, organizing a surprise party for a friend, overcoming fear of heights, learning to do your taxes, stopping smoking and staying with an exercise program, winning a bridge tournament, being a volunteer adult literacy teacher, maintaining three close friendships for over five years, being active in a church group, writing your aging parent each week. Once you have completed the list, share it with your spouse. The spouse can add one to three characteristics that he respects you for. In addition, the spouse can note one to three characteristics he would like you to change or add which would increase his respect for you. You decide if meeting those requests would increase your self-respect.

Next, list attributes that you exhibit in the marriage. Again, try to list at least five, but feel free to write down as many as you like. Examples could include being receptive and responsive to your spouse's touch, being assertive and focused when discussing hard issues, disciplining children effectively as well as being nurturing, doing difficult tasks on your own rather than depending on your spouse, not letting yourself be in the middle between your spouse and his parents, joining a weight reduction and exercise program together, being there—emotionally and practically—for your spouse when she was in crisis, confronting in a loving but direct manner your spouse's avoidance of social interactions with new couples, discussing money management issues, planning couple vacations. After completing the list, share it with him. Urge him to add one to three components that he respects about how you handle yourself in the marriage as well as one to three requests that would increase his respect for how you deal with the marriage. Self-respect and respect for the spouse are based on how you communicate, solve problems, and deal with the challenges of married life.

The next list is what you respect about your spouse. Be genuine and specific in identifying his personal attributes, listing at least five and feeling free to add as many as you like.

Lastly, each of you make a list of what you respect about your marriage. Be aware of both positive attributes and your ability to deal with difficult issues. Examples could include working together to strip old wallpaper and repaint a room, pride in building a children's college fund, sharing frustration, in a non-blaming manner, about an automobile purchase that was a mistake, enjoying entertaining couple friends, sharing chores on weekdays, supporting each other and talking out problems involving parenting, having an exciting sexual relationship, reaching agreements on how to manage a

- Work -
  - technical abilities
- my optimism
- getting Along w/ people /
- relationship w/ Allison, Lola
- MANAging
- good w/ children
- School work I do
- MBA

- Accomplishments on house
- Club together
- Share responsibilities

- Ambition
- Achievements @ work
- CAring for family (mom)
- good w/ children
- great w/ my parents
- dedication to golf
- relationship w/ Rich

- work on house
- Share responsibilities
- Both cook for dinners

from Heather Makgill

difficult in-law situation, being affectionate during good times and bad.

TRUST

When couples think of trust they immediately focus on an extramarital affair and whether trust can be restored. We view trust in a broader perspective and suggest a proactive approach to building and strengthening the trust bond. The essence of trust is the belief that your spouse has your best interest in mind and would not purposefully do something to undermine or hurt you. Every marriage has its disappointments, conflicts, and angers. What destroys trust is not conflict, but the belief that the spouse has intentionally caused the hurt. Trust involves a basic assumption about the type of person your spouse is and how much she values the marital commitment.

Typically, trust issues are not discussed; each spouse assumes an implicit understanding. Trust becomes a crisis only when there is an incident—humiliation in front of family or friends, the discovery of a secret such as an extramarital affair, a child placed for adoption, not graduating from college as claimed, having declared bankruptcy, attempted suicide, or letters portraying you as lazy and irresponsible.

Ideally, before marriage, or early in the marriage, each spouse would state, clearly and specifically, how important trust is and exactly what would constitute a breach of marital trust. When working with couples, Barry suggests each spouse make a "hit below the belt" list. This raises awareness of vulnerable areas and the importance of not using them against the spouse. Honoring this list, even in the middle of an emotionally intense argument, increases the trust bond. We encourage a newly married couple to construct a similar list with an agreement to not hit below the belt.

Issues from the family of origin or personal values sensitize you to areas involving trust. If there were constant fights in your family of origin about money, with accusations of stealing or withholding money, it is crucial to develop clear agreements about money and to trust that those agreements will be honored. A common agreement is that each spouse maintains his own checking account as well as the couple having a joint account. If a spouse had a hidden savings account, this would be a major violation of trust. If your mother had a nine-year affair and everyone in the neighborhood treated your father with pity and condescension, you would need a clear agreement about affairs, respect, and trust.

Issues involving trust are especially relevant to second marriages. If an issue from the first marriage was that the spouse, when angry, would attack his lovemaking style, he has to alert his second wife to the importance of talking about sexual problems in a non-blaming, problem-solving manner. Those discussions are better conducted when dressed and outside the bedroom.

The issue of extramarital affairs is complex, value-laden, and explosive. In theory, people are opposed to extramarital sexuality. In reality, some type of affair will occur in about two-thirds of marriages. The most common type of affair is a "high opportunity-low involvement" male affair which could take place at an out-of-town business meeting or at a massage parlor or with a prostitute. The type of affair that is most disruptive and threatening is the "comparison" affair where more emotional and/or sexual needs are met through the affair than the marriage. This is the most common type of female affair. Since the woman having an affair is a reversal of the double standard, it is more likely to throw the marriage into crisis. A joke in mental health circles is that affairs are good for business.

Extramarital affairs are not a one-dimensional category: there are different types of affairs, motivated by a multitude of factors, having a range of implications for the person and spouse's self-esteem, and different outcomes for the marriage. An affair can be an unplanned, impulsive way to bring excitement to a dull winter; other times it serves as an impetus to leave an unsatisfying marriage. An affair can serve as a means to reinforce attractiveness or self-esteem, a hostile act of revenge, testing whether you are sexually functional, a high opportunity accident, a statement about the need to change your life, a call for help, a way to confront dissatisfaction about emotional or sexual issues. Spouses react with hurt, pain, and a profound sense of distrust. Other spouses might be relieved or not care. For some an affair is the death knell of the marriage, while for others it is the beginning of a revitalized marriage. Human beings are amazingly complex. Marriage and sexuality are two of the most intriguing and individualistic aspects of the human experience.

Exercise Two: Your Trust Bond

Each spouse needs to examine how important trust is, to identify crucial elements of the trust bond and incidents that would disrupt the sense of trust. Do not give socially desirable statements or respond defensively; state what is personally meaningful. For some people trust is a crucial element in marriage; without it they feel insecure and not respected. Others don't consider trust a major element; financial security, couple friends, children, personal autonomy, being part of a community, a house, or a sense of adventure are more valued.

List at least three elements of trust that are particularly important to you. Examples include not lying, sharing important experiences, being sexually faithful, refraining from physical violence, being respectful and supportive in front of children, honoring marital agreements. Examples of events that would disrupt trust include falling in love, humiliating the spouse in front of children or extended family, withholding money, having an ongoing affair, engaging in illegal or unethical activity, revealing an intimate secret, or physically or sexually abusing children.

This can be a disturbing and stressful exercise. It causes couples to confront assumptions and fears. It is particularly distressing if you find the spouse does not respect your needs or has different values concerning the importance or meaning of trust. Being clear about each person's values is better than being "blind-sided" at a later date. Even if you are unable to reach an understanding, at least you know where your spouse stands. As with other exercises, we suggest you write these understandings out and each keep a copy.

Our Personal Agreement About Trust.

Neither Emily nor Barry came from families of origin where there was respect or trust, although neither set of parents had extramarital affairs. Distrust centered around money, power, and control issues. Unfortunately, the distrust was warranted. There were not clear marital agreements and one person did have hidden agendas that subverted the spouse's needs.

Developing and reinforcing trust has been an important issue in our marriage. For Barry, the top elements were establishing agreements and not having hidden agendas. For Emily, they were trusting that Barry had her best interests in mind and would not physically or emotionally intimidate her in order to get his way. Our living situation and Barry's travel provides high opportunity for extramarital affairs, so we established an up-front agreement that neither person would have an affair. This agreement has served us well in reducing suspicion and building trust. That is the advantage of explicit agreements. The disadvantage is that if the agreement is breached you can't say you didn't know, or that it wasn't a big deal. In sharing our agreements, we do not want to come across as sanctimonious. We have experienced a number of incidents where there have been non-communication, hurt feelings, disappointment, and anger. However, it was clear the spouse had not behaved intentionally. Trust for each other and our marital bond adds to self-esteem and marital satisfaction.

INTIMACY

Emotional and sexual intimacy is the special glue that makes marriage worthwhile. Loving and feeling loved is one of life's most nurturing experiences. Emotional intimacy and sexual intimacy are separate, but both are necessary for a successful marriage. About fifty percent of married couples complain of sexual dysfunction or dissatisfaction. Marriage can survive problematic sex, but when a marriage becomes asexual it drains vitality. It is agreed among sex therapists that when sexuality functions well it is a relatively minor element—fifteen to twenty percent of the marriage. The major function of sex is to energize the marital bond. However, when sex is problematic or nonexistent it drains the marriage and can become fifty to seventy-five percent of marital dissatisfaction, including being a leading cause of marital dissolution.

Both emotional and sexual intimacy are necessary, but emotional intimacy is more important. Intimacy is one of the most complex and difficult-to-define psychological phenomena. Clinicians talk about intimacy disorders, that males have less capacity for intimacy, or that one spouse has a greater need for intimacy. Is intimacy the ultimate good—the more the better?

Our view is that intimacy, as with other psychological characteristics, is best viewed as a continuum. One extreme is the emotionally isolated, alienated spouse; the other is the emotionally dependent, needy person (the co-dependent). Neither extreme has the capacity for genuine emotional intimacy. Here are the core components of emotional intimacy:

1. Disclose your attitudes, perceptions, and feelings.
2. Trust yourself and spouse.
3. Share a range of feelings from joy to sadness and anger to contentment.
4. Make long-term commitments and follow through on promises and agreements.
5. Accept yourself and your partner with strengths and weaknesses.

Genuine intimacy is much more than strongly felt loving expressions. Its essence is the ability to maintain emotional connection through difficult and painful times and to honor commitments. In our culture, the strong emotional expressions seen on adult soap operas like ''Dallas'' and ''thirtysomething'' symbolize adult intimacy. Nothing could be further from the truth. Entertainment, whether television, movies, or novels, thrives on conflict and emotional baring of the soul. Emotional intimacy among married couples is less dramatic, but more necessary and vital. It requires talking about and dealing with complex issues that don't end after a two-hour movie, television season, or three-hundred-page novel. The feelings expressed, agreements reached, and secrets shared become an ongoing part of your life. Crucial in an intimate relationship is trusting your spouse to honor feelings and agreements.

The core is reaching a mutually acceptable and comfortable level of intimate relating. Our preference is the ''best friend'' model of emotional intimacy. Each person maintains his or her individuality, rather than their lives being totally intertwined. Yet there are no secrets and the entire range of attitudes, perceptions, and feelings are shared.

Successful marriages can have a different model of emotional intimacy. Some couples maintain greater individuality, more flexibility in what is shared, more individual freedom in managing their lives. Other couples value emotional intimacy with friends, extended family, social, or political groups. They maintain a more distant, but functional and satisfying, marital relationship. Each couple need to develop their way of sharing intimacy, but for a successful marriage there must be emotional intimacy. Otherwise, you run the risk of having a marriage of convenience, which is likely to degenerate into a hollow shell.

Emotional intimacy is not at a constant level; it can and does shift within individuals and couples. For example, there were times in our marriage when we felt particularly intimate, when dealing with a family-related problem or having a couple weekend at a bed and breakfast inn. There were periods of lessened intimacy when Barry was distracted by a professional task or Emily was involved with a home-restoration project. Intimacy does not mean sharing everything all the time; this suffocates individuality. However, sharing thoughts and feelings is a vital component of a successful marriage.

Is emotional intimacy a prerequisite to sexual intimacy? Most theorists, clinicians, ministers, and your mother would answer "yes." However, for most couples the answer is "preferably, but not necessarily." Sexuality has many functions—a shared pleasure, a means to strengthen intimacy, a tension reducer. The most satisfying sexual experiences involve both partners sharing emotional intimacy and being desirous, aroused, and orgasmic. That's what movies and books like to show. How often does it happen? If a couple are sexually functional and lucky, this scenario might occur once every four times they make love. If they are an extremely sexually functional couple, it might even occur forty percent of the time. For most couples, if they have one or two particularly intimate and sexually exciting experiences a month, they are doing well.

What does this say about the role of sexual intimacy in marriage? Couples—fueled by media myths—have unrealistic expectations about marital sexuality. Sexuality can and should nurture the marital bond, but "dynamite" sex is the exception rather than the rule for even the best of couples. Sex does not have to be equally satisfying to be worthwhile. Variability is the norm in sexual expression. Intimate sexuality is the most fulfilling, but sex is like food: various and serving different functions. If every time you sat down to eat you got out china and crystal and had a four-course gourmet meal, this would become boring and distasteful. Cooking hamburgers on the grill, getting Chinese takeout, or making an elaborate salad, can be enjoyable. In the same manner, sexuality can be a "quickie" intercourse, a way to make up after a disagreement, a tension reducer after a difficult day, a sexual release to help you get to sleep, a way to have fun and be silly, a mediocre or poor experience, or a sharing of your most erotic, passionate feelings.

In some ways, the least intimate thing you can do sexually is have intercourse late at night. Initiating requires little risk:

you're already in bed with clothes off—you can just reach over, touch your partner, see if he's interested. Most couples equate intercourse with sex—it's the "normal" sexual behavior. Making a sexual date is a risk. Engaging in pleasuring or making a sexual request is more intimate than "sticking it in." Sexuality is more than genitals, intercourse, and the few seconds of orgasm. Sexual intimacy includes affectionate touching both inside and outside the bedroom; nondemand pleasuring, both dressed and nude; sensual experiences, like bathing together and whole body caresses; giving and receiving genital stimulation to build erotic feelings; multiple stimulation during intercourse; and a warm and connected afterplay. Sexuality is an expression of how you feel about yourself as a person and how you express yourselves as a couple. Sexuality can be intimate whether or not it includes intercourse. You can have functional and orgasmic sex that contains no intimacy. Theoretically, clinically, and personally we value sexuality that is intimate, but it's important to realize that not all marital sexuality is or need be intimate.

Exercise Three: Emotional Intimacy

Perhaps the most crucial element of intimacy is self-disclosure. There are many types and levels of communication. Spouses talk about jobs, chores, houses, children, money, politics, sports, community gossip. What is to be revealed in this exercise is something emotionally important and personal. It might mean disclosing a secret, a childhood trauma or victory, a hope or dream, a fear or vulnerability, a request for help. Sharing something personal allows you to be vulnerable and emotionally intimate. Decide what you want to share and why you are sharing it. Be sure its purpose is to deepen emotional intimacy, not as a hostile act to demoralize the spouse or a way of shifting responsibility from you to her. The motivation is to increase emotional intimacy; there should be no hidden agendas.

Wait a day or two before the spouse's self-disclosure. Don't be competitive. Share what is personal and special.

What happens in too many marriages is an emotional deadening; you are no longer sharing a life together, merely functioning in the same space. The best remedy is keeping emotional contact, and the best mechanism for that is self-disclosure.

Exercise Four: Sexual Intimacy

Sex does not equal intercourse. We would like you to experience that through this exercise, which will focus on exploration, nongenital sensuality, and playful, as opposed to orgasm-oriented, genital pleasuring. In other words, no intercourse or orgasm. With those performance demands removed and no goal orientation, can you be open to pleasure and sexual intimacy?

We suggest a pleasurer-pleasuree (giver-recipient) format. Let the woman go first. The giver can explore her partner's entire body from the hair on his head to the soles of his feet. Instead of trying to second-guess what he wants, touch for yourself. Enjoy the giving process. If something is uncomfortable or hurts, he can tell you; otherwise, he lies back, closes his eyes, and takes in pleasurable sensations. Give yourself permission to look at his body. Explore it with your hands, arms, palms, tips of fingers, tongue, lips, without performance pressure. Find at least two parts of his body you find especially attractive and enjoy touching. After you've explored the back, have him roll over and explore his front. Feel free to look at and playfully touch his scrotum, shaft of the penis, and penile glans. If he becomes erect, enjoy that, but don't feel a pressure to respond to his erection. Most women (and men) view an erection as a sexual demand, not as a natural response to touching and pleasure. Enjoy exploring and playing with his body, including his penis.

When she has finished sensual pleasuring, he can make one or two requests for additional touching—for pleasure, not orgasm. Sexual intimacy includes sharing what feels good and making requests.

You can switch roles or make a date to reciprocate the

pleasuring at another time. For many men, the hardest part of being giver is to do slow, gentle, rhythmic caressing for pleasure rather than "working to turn her on." Remember, touch for yourself—enjoy looking at and exploring her whole body. Don't focus on the breasts or vulva. Traditionally, it has not been considered feminine to make sexual requests or guide your partner. Men were supposed to be the sexual experts; it was a sign of sexual prowess and masculinity to be a sophisticated lover. Give yourself permission now to make verbal or nonverbal requests. Sexual intimacy involves being open, sharing pleasure, requesting, and developing a couple sexual style. In subsequent experiences you can experiment with powder or lotion, mutual pleasuring, integrating intercourse into the pleasuring process, experimenting with different scenarios and positions. The essence of sexual intimacy is giving and receiving pleasure-oriented touching.

Janet and Roger. There are no perfect marriages, but Janet and Roger are proud of their growth as a couple. They married twelve years ago; this was Janet's second marriage and Roger's first. Their marriage has not only survived but thrived despite a number of difficulties that would have devastated other couples. Janet's daughter was seven when they married and she never developed a positive attachment to Roger (a loss for both of them). Three months after the marriage, Janet's sister died in a car accident caused by a drunk driver. A year later, Roger was laid off and it took seven months for him to find a suitable job. Janet had two miscarriages before they had a daughter. Roger's father had an incapacitating stroke and died eleven months later. Janet was sexually harassed at work and the grievance took two years to settle.

Marriage is a process of sharing life together with joys and sorrows, successes and difficulties. Key to a marital bond is dealing with hard and sad issues without falling into the psychological traps of depression and avoidance on one hand and acting out through drinking or an affair on the other.

Two things kept Janet and Roger's marital bond intact. They loved to dance and had a dance group they went to at least once a week. Even when things were especially stressful or difficult, they made sure to save at least one night for dancing. They needed this time to reenergize themselves and their marital bond. The second coping technique was going to dinner on Sunday night by themselves. Janet and Roger were a social couple who did most activities with other couples and families. Their house buzzed with people and activities. Their children's friends loved coming over because there was so much going on. They had a standing Sunday night babysitter so they could have an evening to themselves to talk about issues, discuss the coming week, and share emotional intimacy. They got home in time for Roger to read to the children and put them to bed while Janet took the babysitter home. The evening and weekend ended with pleasurable lovemaking.

Over the twelve years, their sense of respect and trust has grown. At the beginning, Janet was clearly the dominant partner, partly because so many decisions, such as living in a neighborhood with a good elementary school, were influenced by her daughter's needs. A key element in marriage is to establish a sense of equity so there is not a power imbalance. This is important in establishing roles, dividing chores and tasks, decision making (especially about money), and acknowledging each person's contributions. Janet came from a traditional family where male and female roles were completely different and segregated. She had no desire to repeat that pattern in her marriage. Roger's family preached equality, but Roger felt that his mother dominated his father. Roger himself had a tendency to be the "good guy," and fall into the same trap. Janet did not respect him when he did what she wanted to keep the peace; she desired an equitable partnership, not someone who would placate her and give in. Janet and Roger learned to express feelings, discuss alternatives, make requests, and reach agreements each could live with. Roger needed to state his feelings and needs, take a stand, and negotiate harder. This was not easy, but when he did, his self-respect increased as did Janet's respect for him.

A core element in their marital bond was trust. Janet's first husband accused her of not trusting him. She didn't, and was right in her judgment. He had taken $4,000 from their joint checking account to buy cocaine. Janet didn't worry about that with Roger, but was concerned about whether she could count on him in an emotionally confrontative situation. Janet had a conflict with an aunt regarding wedding arrangements for a cousin. Roger started out trying to be conciliatory and rational, but realized that this was an emotional dispute, not a matter of rational decision making. Roger took on the role of Janet's supporter. Knowing she could trust Roger's support allowed Janet to stand up to her aunt. Eventually an agreement was reached that was acceptable. Trust does not mean always agreeing with or supporting your spouse. It does mean not disparaging her in front of others or intentionally undercutting her. Trust means believing your spouse cares about you and has your best interests in mind. Their trust bond was tested and grew stronger.

Sex did not come easily for Janet and Roger. Roger was an early ejaculator and Janet had low sexual desire, although once involved, arousal and orgasm were fairly easy. Both hoped the other would cure the problem. Waiting for the spouse to change is certain to cause frustration and disappointment. Each person must take responsibility for his or her sexuality.

There are many harmful myths about early ejaculation from the idea that it is a sign of hostility to techniques for reducing arousal, like biting your lips or thinking of your mother-in-law. Early ejaculation is caused by the habit of combining high arousal and anxiety. The key is to maintain arousal while increasing awareness and comfort. The couple need to communicate about sexual feelings and establish a regular intercourse frequency. They will not develop ejaculatory control if intercourse is once a week; learning ejaculatory control is a gradual process that takes most couples between three and six months of concentrated effort. It was more difficult for Roger and Janet because they argued over the meaning of the sexual problem and she became easily discouraged, which further inhibited desire. After two unsuccessful attempts to turn the problem around by themselves, they sought couple sex therapy. The therapy lasted eight sessions and was of great value. The process of disclosing sexual thoughts and feelings, learning the stop-start technique for ejaculatory control, designing sexual scenarios to increase desire, sharing intimate feelings and sensual touching outside the bedroom, and affirming the value of the marriage facilitated a healthier sexual as well as emotional bond. Sexual feelings do not occur in a vacuum. Janet and Roger found couple sex therapy the best eight hours they invested in the marriage.

NURTURING THE MARITAL BOND

Even after twenty-five years of marriage, our bond continues to need attention and reinforcement. You can't neglect marriage. Respect, trust, and intimacy need to be valued by both people. In our culture, the focus has been to find the right person to marry. In truth, creating and maintaining an intimate, stable marriage is by far the more complex and difficult task. As a culture we value the symbol of marriage, not the process of living as a married couple. The person who respects herself, trusts her motivation, and is able to be emotionally and sexually intimate will have high self-esteem and a satisfying marital bond. Self-esteem and marriage cannot rest on their laurels even after fifty years. The marital bond is an ongoing process that needs to be valued and nurtured.

FIVE

Couple Agreements and Positive Influence

The two psychological strategies we most recommend are setting aside couple time and making an agreement. This chapter focuses on how couples make and implement successful agreements.

We remember an aunt at our wedding encouraging us, especially Emily, to learn to compromise: ''Marriage requires compromises.'' Marital compromises result in frustration and stagnation, they can sink a marriage into a morass of dissatisfaction. Conflicting feelings and wants are a natural part of marriage. Trying to compromise issues away won't work.

We advocate an agreement process in which each spouse states feelings and perceptions, generates alternatives, addresses the costs and benefits of each alternative, negotiates a viable agreement, and creates a system to monitor and implement a successful change. A viable agreement meets the needs of each individual as well as couple needs. In our marriage, we have agreements about mundane issues like who does grocery shopping and who is responsible for cooking. We make agreements about major issues like a five-year plan for restoring and decorating our hundred-year-old house. We've never had a perfect agreement that met our needs completely and had no drawbacks. However, we have had [illegible] of good agreements that help resolve issues. An agreement usually meets one partner's needs more than the other's, but with several couple agreements each spouse feels a sense of equity. For example, Emily values old houses, antiques, and gardens. She was the prime person in choosing our house because her interests and needs were stronger. Barry had input, especially about the location, because for him milieu and scenery are particularly important. Vacations are a different matter. Barry loves to plan and anticipate trips so he takes prime responsibility. Emily has a veto power over places she would be uncomfortable going to, as well as preferences for what she wants to see and do.

Inherent in the concept of couple agreements is the positive influence process. This is in contrast to getting your way by any means, including coercion. In traditional marriages, men would withhold money and women would withhold sex as a means of punishing the spouse and getting her or him to give in. The coercive demand process said, "Do it my way; do it now or you'll be punished." The positive influence process says, "These are my feelings and wants, here is my request; let us work together to reach an agreement that is good for both of us." There is no threat of retaliation or punishment. In coercive demands, it's as if the couple were at war and each tries to win the battle. In a positive influence process the goal is a stable and satisfying marriage with agreements being an important link in the marital bond. When Barry is working with dysfunctional couples locked in a power struggle, he says, "You are so intent on winning this battle you don't realize the war is causing the loss of your marriage."

The basis for couple agreements is respect and trust. This requires an equitable balance of power because without it the concept of positive influence is a sham. In a marriage where there is a giant discrepancy in power and/or one spouse builds ego by disparaging the other, good agreements cannot be made. For couple agreements to be viable, there has to be a "level playing field." You need to trust that your motivations, and those of your spouse, are to promote self-esteem and the marital bond.

Larry and Gail. Larry and Gail were in their late forties, experiencing the stresses of being responsible for parents and children, a common problem for couples from thirty to sixty. Larry's father had died four years before; his mother was seventy-nine and in good health. Gail's parents were alive, but both her eighty-two-year-old father and seventy-nine-year-old mother were in poor health. Larry and Gail had an unmarried twenty-six-year-old daughter, a twenty-four-year-old son who was married and had a six-month-old daughter, and a seventeen-year-old daughter who was entering senior year of high school. Larry was the parts manager for a large car dealership and Gail sold residential real estate on a part-time basis. Larry had always made a significantly higher income and complained that Gail did not carry her share. Gail enjoyed combining parenting and working. She was one of the most successful part-time agents in her office, but limited work so she could help the daughter with college plans, be a back-up caretaker for the grandchild, and be available to help her aging parents and mother-in-law. Gail resented Larry's assertion that she didn't carry her weight. Gail contributed more in all areas other than income. Larry's salary was $45,000 with additional bonuses and perks, while Gail's real estate commissions totaled almost $30,000. With a mortgage, bills, and a daughter preparing to enter college, finances were tight. Larry resented this, and placed the blame on Gail. Whether discussing washing dishes, paying bills, or where to go on vacation, the dominant theme was Larry's sense of entitlement because he made more money. He gave Gail little to no credit for her contributions to the family or finances. He was glad to leave contact with his mother to Gail because he felt he'd "outgrown" her. He also felt too young to take the grandfather role and "burned out" from parenting, so he was minimally involved with their seventeen-year-old daughter. Larry's life revolved around work, anger about money, and his golf game.

Gail was overburdened with responsibilities, but felt emotionally well-connected, especially to friends, adult children, and grandchild. She found parenting adolescents particularly frustrating; nonetheless she remained involved with her daughter's life and plans, and felt alienated by Larry's unreasonableness regarding money and family issues.

Larry and Gail had a far from perfect pattern of resolving problems. They informally divided their lives into domains. The person in charge of that domain made the decision, with little input from the spouse. Recently, over the past two years, this system broke down as Larry became more strident and insistent that, since he carried the financial burdens, his vote was the one that counted. Gail was resentful, but placating. She complained to friends that Larry must be going through a midlife crisis. She gave up trying to influence him positively. When he coerced her to do things his way, her agitation increased but she maintained silence.

The money problem reached crisis proportions when Larry insisted Gail not buy baby furniture for their grandchild. Gail had promised this to her son and daughter-in-law and had taken great satisfaction in shopping and finding a bargain. Gail was not going to allow Larry to control her life and negate her promise to the grandchild. Neither did she want an emotional scene, with his screaming and her crying, charges and countercharges hurled. Instead, she wrote Larry a letter. The letter detailed the issues around power, money, and decision-making. She acknowledged Larry's past and present contributions to the family, listed her contributions, and asked Larry to be aware of and acknowledge these. She stated how important it was to buy the grandchild's furniture, and suggested that she use her next commission check for that and other family needs. She ended the letter with an invitation to go on a canoe outing that Sunday and discuss money issues.

Although suspicious, Larry was taken with Gail's invitation. As he reread the letter and thought about the points Gail raised, he became aware how one-sided his view had been. Sunday it rained, which spoiled canoeing, so they went to their favorite Chinese restaurant and sat at a back table so they'd have privacy, and talked for four hours. Rather than falling into the trap of defensiveness and blaming, each took responsibility for changing his/her attitudes and behavior. Larry acknowledged Gail's contributions, agreed to limit golfing to twice a week, reinvolve himself with his mother and adolescent daughter, play with the grandchild, and eliminate or at least significantly reduce his angry tirades and putdowns. Gail agreed to adhere to a budget, to not speak of Larry as a tyrant or second-class father or to describe herself as a "golf widow," and to initiate affectionate and sexual interchanges. They did not expect changes to be miraculous or easy, but felt they now had a "level playing field" to discuss money and reach couple agreements.

EXAMPLES OF THE AGREEMENT PROCESS

For this process to work, each spouse must take responsibility to honor his or her end of the agreement. They cannot fall into the tit-for-tat trap of saying, "I won't do my part if my partner doesn't do his part." Each spouse independently assumes responsibility to carry out his end of the agreement. The reward is increased self-respect and better marital functioning.

Nagging or threatening will not facilitate the agreement process. The spouse is encouraged to ask for help in following through. If you do not believe your spouse is living up to the agreement, say what you observe and how you are feeling, but do not nag or threaten. Encouragement and reinforcement is more likely to promote successful implementation of change.

A common area for agreement involves household chores. There is never enough time, energy, or motivation for chores. It is important to develop an equitable system and not harbor grudges. Couples are encouraged to choose chores in which they feel competent and interested. These can be along traditional gender roles or be a reversal. In our marriage, Emily is the cook because she enjoys and is good at it while Barry is better at finances and investments—a traditional set of roles. On the other hand, Emily does repair work and the lawn because of interest and competence, and charge of grocery shopping and dishes. To avoid ry cooks once a week and Emily does grocery e a month.

If one spouse feels the other is not carrying his fair share, instead of complaining and undercutting make a new agreement or revise the old one. Make specific, positive requests for change instead of attacking the spouse. Remember to make "I" statements about feelings, perceptions, and requests rather than "you" statements that blame or attack. Agreements are about sharing, cooperating, and working together rather than competing, disparaging, and getting your own way. This sounds idealistic but most couples find that it works. Good agreements get things done and move the relationship forward. You get what you want, but not at the expense of your spouse—a "win-win" not a "win-lose" situation. Never agree to something that is not in your best interest or that doesn't have at least a fifty-fifty chance of success. Good agreements break an impasse and move the process toward resolution. Agreements increase a couple's confidence in their ability to deal with issues. As clients tell Barry, "There was no great resolution, but we feel better because we talked it out and came up with a plan."

POSITIVE INFLUENCE PROCESS

The positive influence process is integral to couple agreements. When Barry explains the importance of trying to influence a spouse positively, couples say it sounds good, but it's so different from what they typically do that it won't work. Couples are used to complaining, saying it's the same old thing, working around or manipulating. You get friends or relatives on your side, do it your way, and ignore the spouse and his needs. Other couples make a pretense of communicating, but the stronger spouse decides she's going to do it her way and "running it by" the husband is a pretense. Marriage becomes a power struggle; each person has his sphere of influence where the other keeps hands off. During conflict, there are threats and counterthreats. This results in difficult marriages and is destructive for self-esteem.

When the couple believe in and utilize the positive influence process, each attempts to state feelings, perceptions, and desires. In a respectful, intimate marriage feelings are validated, not argued over. Share information and perceptions so you can deal constructively with issues. In exploring alternatives, the goal is not to get your way or convince your spouse that you have a better idea, but to find an alternative or series of alternatives that address the issue and take into account both people's needs. The focus is on dealing with issues and moving along the couple process. Each person makes an effort to reach an agreement that serves his needs and the needs of the couple. In the positive influence process you want to get your needs met, but *not* at the expense of the relationship. In power struggles, the couple fight to win the battle, but they lose the war for the relationship. There are very few issues important enough to risk your marital bond. Reach a mutually acceptable agreement that promotes self-esteem and the marital bond.

David and Marsha. The decision of how to celebrate their fifteenth wedding anniversary was a challenge to David and Marsha's positive influence and agreement process. David was not a big believer in celebration, and the previous year had been a difficult one financially. He was concerned about who would watch their twelve-year-old daughter and ten-year-old son. Events such as anniversaries, birthdays, and holidays were special for Marsha and she resented David's inclination to ignore the occasion and apologize afterward. She loved to anticipate an event and later to recall special moments. This gave her almost as much pleasure as the actual time. She wanted a special fifteenth anniversary celebration, which she assured David could be enjoyable without being expensive. Marsha arranged for her parents to drive from their retirement condominium in the mountains of North Carolina to watch the children. In turn, she and David would the condominium and go hiking, one of his favorite s. David had to admit this was a creative idea and was willing to participate, not just passively go along.

Over fifteen years of marriage, David had learned a number of important psychological lessons. Listening to Marsha and her feelings and sharing his feelings and perceptions was a prerequisite for reaching satisfactory agreements. Professionally, David was a troubleshooter—quickly assessing a problem and utilizing the right resources and technology to solve it. In his business, feelings and perceptions counted little, but he was aware that they counted heavily in marriage and that sharing them was necessary for marital intimacy. He realized that the most practical and logical alternative was often not the healthiest solution psychologically. He vividly remembered his boss doing a cost-benefit analysis of child care arrangements and deciding that having two child care people, one of them a live-in, was the optimal arrangement. David valued the privacy and integrity of his home life, and could not tolerate a live-in person. Even more important, he found great emotional satisfaction in giving baths to his children, reading bedtime stories, and hearing their prayers. How do you weigh that using the scale of time and money? Psychological satisfaction is more important than logical arrangements, efficiency, and cost. David found that the best way to influence Marsha was to listen to and respect her. When she felt attended to, she was open to David's thoughts and plans. When he told her why something was important to him, she gave it serious consideration. When David was open to Marsha's suggestions and modifications, the agreement they reached would not only work but be satisfying.

In comparison to fifteen years before, Marsha was sophisticated and realistic. As a young woman, she was a believer that communication and love would cause everything to work perfectly. She still preferred being optimistic to being cynical, but knew that life could be complex and difficult. Love and good intentions were not enough. Marsha continued to believe in the power of communication, but realized its limitations. Seven years before, when she'd had a disagreement with her mother about parenting, she had been convinced that if she could communicate effectively they would reach an understanding about what her mother did when the children stayed with her. However, the problem was not lack of communication, listening to feelings, or being assertive. The problem was content. They disagreed. No matter how much time and energy was spent in discussion, the disagreement would not go away. Finally, Marsha had to bite the bullet and say that these were her children, she was responsible for their well-being, and her mother had to do it Marsha's way. Her mother agreed, but was not won over nor would she listen to Marsha's attempts to smooth things out. This was a painful but valuable lesson.

Marsha learned to deal with hard issues and be satisfied with imperfect agreements. She prioritized what was important, whether that involved decorating the house or balancing time for children, couple time, work, individual time, and extended family time. It pained her to see one of her best friends change from a romantic idealist to a bitter cynic because she felt that her husband no longer loved her when he didn't do what she wanted. The friend saw life's disappointments and struggles as the failure of love. Feeling loving toward and emotionally connected to David was critical. Marsha realized that love and communication were necessary, but not enough. Facing difficult issues and reaching understandings and agreements was critical. One of the most important aspects of a couple agreement is to monitor it so gains are maintained.

David and Marsha discussed and planned for their fifteenth wedding anniversary. It was Marsha's suggestion that each plan something that reflected the past fifteen years and something that looked to the future, keeping the plans a surprise. David was anticipating the four days, and Marsha enjoyed preparing her surprise. But David was uncomfortable with surprises; he wanted to be sure Marsha would enjoy his plans. She accepted this as his style, rather than trying to talk him into doing it her way. He suggested spending a night camping and, by the campfire, looking at pictures they had taken during the years. To symbolize the future he and Marsha would create a joint fantasy of an ideal life in ten years, when they'd be a couple again. Marsha was enthusiastic, but had modifications, one of which she shared with David; that they write down plans so they could look at them in ten years. The addition she did not share was making the campout the kind of sensual/sexual experience they weren't comfortable with fifteen years before.

Marsha's plans, which she did keep a surprise, were to cook the same dinner she'd made for their first anniversary—she loved to cook gourmet meals as much as David loved eating them—but this time she was going to involve him in the food preparation, something she'd like more of in the future. She also bought new lingerie and a scented lotion for a body massage. In the future, she wanted sensuous touching to be an integral part of lovemaking.

Marsha and David celebrated their first fifteen years and set the stage for the next fifteen. Positive influence and couple agreements were two of their valued marital resources.

REACHING POSITIVE AGREEMENTS

Most couples think of agreements in the context of dealing with disagreements and problems. Although this is crucial and will be addressed in the second exercise, making positive agreements is necessary and beneficial. Examples of positive agreements include going to dinner as a couple at least twice a month, setting aside two hours of couple time on a Sunday afternoon, doing household or yard chores in tandem, watching the children one night a week while the spouse goes out with friends, being sure when visiting in-laws that the spouse has a good time, planning a family outing once a week, having a family workday twice a month, being sexual sometime other than late at night, going as a family to religious services, the spouse being responsive to your needs when you're feeling low, going out with another couple or having them to your house for dinner at least once a month. The marital bond needs special times and attention. It is too easy to take the spouse and marriage for granted. Positive agreements are a means to insure nurturing marital experiences.

Exercise One: Positive Agreements

Before making new agreements, list your present agreements, whether formal or informal. Many couples approach this exercise with the belief that they don't have couple agreements, but when they talk about it realize that there are a number of informal understandings that enhance the marriage. Examples include the husband getting the paper, making coffee, and bringing it to bed; giving a back rub or foot massage after a stressful day; playing doubles tennis on Sunday afternoon; going to lunch after the children's soccer game; having pizza and beer at one A.M. after wallpapering a room; a Wednesday night bridge game; snuggling on the couch and watching your favorite TV show after the children are in bed; when visiting the wife's parents, taking two hours as a couple to go for a hike along the river.

This exercise is to establish at least two new positive couple agreements. What special experiences or activities would reenergize the marital bond? Feel free to state needs and make requests. These could be major, such as asking your spouse to watch the kids two nights a week so you can take a course or training program. Or something mundane, such as greeting you at the door with a kiss or talking in bed for five minutes before going to sleep. You could request something of symbolic significance, such as bringing flowers home instead of a sixpack of beer. An emotionally meaningful request might be to talk about your spouse as if she were your best friend. Or you could be very practical—ask for an agreement to share cooking or dusting.

You could create a list of five requests, and have your spouse choose one or two to implement. Positive agreements boost self-esteem and energize the marital bond. Each agreement has value in itself. Stay away from tit-for-tat agreements. The danger of these is they become bogged down in arguments about one spouse not doing his part so the other spouse won't do hers. Tit-for-tat agreements result in paralysis. Positive agreements result in increased satisfaction.

After reaching an agreement, decide how to implement it. Good intentions are not enough. Some system—formal or informal, oral or written—needs to be in place to monitor and successfully implement the agreement. Our favorite system is to put the agreement someplace easily seen (like the door of the refrigerator or the nightstand), and once a week, on a walk or talking over the kitchen table, review how well the agreement is going. Develop your own system, but be sure you have something, otherwise the likely outcome is that the agreement, no matter how positive and motivated you were at the time you made it, will lapse into disuse. If it was important enough to make, you owe it to yourself and your marriage to reap the benefits of successful implementation.

Exercise Two: Problem-Solving Agreements

This is the more difficult type of agreement, but the more important. Everyday hassles and problems reduce self-esteem and tear at the marital fabric. Making an agreement can resolve the problem, build self-esteem, and solidify the marital bond. Of course, not all agreements will be successful. There are agreements that are good for self-esteem, but difficult for the marriage. Other agreements can be beneficial for the marital bond and one person's self-esteem, but be of little benefit for the spouse. It's important to be sure that an agreement is not harmful. Sacrificing self-esteem for the marriage is not wise.

Start by reviewing old agreements about difficult issues. This is to be aware of what has worked or failed in the past, not to refight old battles or gain retribution for bad agreements. There are several traps couples fall into: one spouse is a relentless negotiator and the other gives in; the couple talk the issue to death without resolution; they settle for "feel good" agreements that duck the difficult issues; agreements are made, but not followed; one spouse gets her way, but the other spouse's passivity subverts the agreement. Do you fall into these or similar traps? Reach and implement successful problem-solving agreements that do not repeat the traps of the past.

We suggest that each spouse identify two difficult areas in which to develop a problem-solving agreement through the positive influence process. Be aware of past traps and focus on making a good, present agreement. Begin by stating feelings and perceptions about the problem. Listen in a respectful and caring manner to your spouse, especially her fears and concerns regarding motivation. Be clear about your motivation; stay away from manipulation and hidden agendas. The goal is to resolve the issue, but not at the expense of the spouse or marital bond. You are not trying to put something over on your spouse or get your way at her expense. In considering alternatives, be open to the spouse's suggestions and modifications rather than trying to force your ideas. Reach a mutually acceptable agreement. Be sure it addresses the concerns of both, even though it's not perfect. It has an excellent chance of success if you both follow through.

EXAMPLES OF COUPLE AGREEMENTS

The husband was upset and frustrated by the pattern of the family's weekends. There was almost no discretionary time and he felt continually on call. He was a middle-level manager with a forty-five-hour work week who needed weekends to reenergize himself. He requested a weekend schedule that was less structured and allowed more freedom. Since his wife worked full time, weekends were the time for chores, children's activities, and family time. She feared he would retreat to the couch and drink beer, which is what he had done before they had children. He assured her that this was not his intention. He wanted his life to be more than that of a worker, householder, and family man. He wanted something special for himself as well as couple time. He resented always feeling on duty, and not being appreciated. His wife not only understood his feelings, but shared them. This served as a basis for the psychological and practical negotiation to restructure time to allow for personal space and fun.

Twice a month he had Saturday afternoon off and once a month she had Saturday morning and once a month Sunday morning off. He realized that it was not so much the time he needed as the feeling that it was okay to enjoy his personal agenda. This agreement reduced alienation and resentment. He viewed his wife as an understanding, supportive friend, not his keeper. The agreement worked better for him, but she learned two things. She could respect him and trust that he was an adult with mature needs, and give up her old view of him as self-centered. Secondly, she was aware of her tendency to be a martyr who gave more than she received. She learned to make her needs known and negotiate hard for an equitable system of organizing children's activities, chores, work, individual time, and couple time.

Our second example is a traditionally organized family where the husband worked a sixty-hour week and the wife worked twenty hours while doing most of the child care and house maintenance. She was suffering from low self-esteem and was intimidated by his gruff responses to requests. He believed that, since he worked hard and made more money, he shouldn't have to be hassled about household and parenting matters. This is a pattern in many marriages. They were at an impasse. He seemed oblivious to the complexity of the problems. She was hurt and depressed that he couldn't understand her feelings or see issues from her perspective. When she tried to assert herself, she felt beaten and gave up.

She read about a technique she thought was applicable. She composed a five-page letter that did not attack him but stated her feelings and desires. At the end she said she wanted to reach understandings and agreements that would bolster self-esteem. She did not want to fight or engage in tit-for-tat arguments, but to acknowledge each person's contributions and reach equitable agreements about money, household, and child care concerns. She suggested they set aside two hours Sunday afternoon to begin the dialogue. He was surprised to get the letter and even more surprised by the contents. It was her turn to be surprised on Saturday when she got a four-page letter starting with all the things about her that he admired and valued, but stated his fears that she wanted him to make dramatic changes (like quitting his job).

In discussing practical and financial realities, they were relieved to discover that neither wanted a dramatic life change nor were there hidden agendas. As the children got older they would reorganize their lives, but at this point the present system made the most sense. What they needed was to acknowledge each other's contributions, change how off-work time and child care were organized, and have more couple time. They were so busy fighting—she for self-esteem and against a sense of depression and worthlessness, and he for his career and against her hassles and dissatisfactions—that they had been too defensive to ask for what they needed. He loved and valued her, and this needed to be expressed. He wanted to achieve a better balance—his entire self-esteem was based on career achievements. Especially crucial was to enjoy his children when they were five and two. When his career enabled him to attend to them, they would not be as open to the fathering he offered. Parenting a five-year-old is a process; she can't be told to wait five years until a career goal is achieved. One agreement this couple reached was that she would have a night out and he'd be home at six ready to parent.

Develop agreements that enhance self-esteem, build the couple bond, and can be successfully implemented. The ability to make and follow through on couple agreements is a valuable resource in intimate, stable marriages.

CLOSING THOUGHTS

No matter how often we talk about communication and problem-solving skills or emphasize that each couple need to develop their own style, we hear people say that if they only loved each other this would be unnecessary. Couple agreements and the positive influence process cannot substitute for a lack of intimacy. However, the most intimate, loving, sexual marriage will degenerate if the couple is not able to reach understandings and agreements.

Self-esteem and marital satisfaction blossoms in a milieu that promotes marital agreement. The couple will survive difficult times if they solve problems and create agreements that address issues and dissatisfactions. Individual self-esteem and the couple bond are nurtured by successful agreements. Realizing that you can deal directly and honestly, without fear of manipulation or intimidation, builds trust. Stating feelings and needs and being listened to in a respectful, caring manner is validating. Agreements are important whether dealing with mundane or crucial issues, either to solve problems or to enhance the marriage.

SIX

Negative Feelings and Difficult Issues

There is a promise in the novel/movie *Love Story*: "Love means never having to say you're sorry." Why can't love and marriage be like the movies? The reality is that all marriages encounter negative feelings and difficult issues. Even in the best of marriages, the couple say they're sorry at least forty times a year. A constant refrain in couples therapy is, "No one ever told me marriage would be this hard."

The focus of this chapter is the hard work that underscores intimate marriages. Most marriage books are upbeat, simplistic, and promise too much. Problems and solutions seem to be taken from half-hour sitcoms, not from the complex lives of couples Barry sees clinically or that we know personally. The marital bond needs continual attention and nurturing. Keeping a marriage vital requires a commitment to individual and couple growth. Issues and problems emerge that require the couple to develop new, improved agreements.

There are two poisons that work against marriage. The most common is neglect. A couple have been together anywhere from five to fifty-five years and assume they don't need to think through or talk out issues and problems. The marriage stagnates, and the resulting dissatisfaction and frustration causes lower self-esteem. The more virulent poison is hostility and alienation. The couple experience an incident concerning children, finances, sexual difficulty, in-law problems, or moving, which festers and becomes a full-blown chronic problem. We have never known a couple who did not experience conflicts, difficulties, and regrets over past incidents and decisions. Difficult issues are inherent in the complex process of marriage. Some conflicts could have been prevented if the couple thought about, talked out, and negotiated a mutually acceptable agreement. Other issues cannot be readily resolved. No matter how much talk or planning, some problems cannot be avoided. The key is to not allow resentment to grow and cause alienation. If a business failure results in a family move that turns out to be a disaster, it can be dealt with by problem-solving rather than falling into a guilt-blame cycle of retribution.

What are the most difficult feelings? Anger is first on most people's list. We agree that anger is a difficult emotion, but believe the most destructive emotion is hopelessness. If you give up on the process of talking with and influencing your spouse, you feel perpetually depressed about the marriage. Giving up on your marriage but sharing the same house is a very difficult way to live. Unless you build a life totally apart from the marriage, self-esteem will continue to plummet.

EMILY'S MOTHER: A PERSONAL NOTE

Two generations ago, women had few choices. They were to marry and stay married no matter what. Emily's mother, Jeannette, married Ralph at twenty and stayed married for fifty-three years until a particularly violent incident caused her adult children to intervene. Ralph entered a nursing home. At his funeral six years later, Jeannette was objective and realistic in her assessment: "Ralph was a tyrant and a very difficult man to live with. He was a better father than husband. He never valued a wife and marriage—he took them as his due." Both Emily and Barry admired Jeannette because she constructed a life apart from the marriage. She enjoyed work and parenting, was a voracious reader, and became an excellent grandmother, an especially important person for our three children.

The three years she lived alone before ill health forced her into a nursing home were the happiest of her life. She demonstrated that she could manage independently. She believed women were as good or better than men—she was a feminist before feminism.

Jeannette's views on self-esteem and marriage had a great deal of influence on us and this book, although she would not agree with much of what we've written. She did not believe that a husband and wife could reach satisfying agreements. Jeannette viewed marriage as a competition between a man and a woman, with the man having an unfair advantage because he made more money and got away with unilateral decisions.

Jeannette applauded work and life options now available to women, but believed marriage remained an inequitable arrangement. She saw marriage as a struggle for dominance in which each side staked out his or her territory. We believe this approach is detrimental to the self-esteem of both women and men. Jeannette's generation had marriages that were stable, but unsatisfying. This chapter is dedicated to her, with the hope that future generations can learn to deal with negative feelings and difficult issues in a respectful, equitable manner, and create marriages that are both satisfying and stable.

SETTING THE STAGE

New couples are so eager for love to last that they try to avoid negative feelings and conflicts. This is self-defeating. We encourage discussion of difficult issues during the premarital period. Couples have to learn to deal with negative feelings and hard issues; courting is not the time to pretend to be perfect or willing to do anything for love. Nor is it the time to play the dating game of being hard to get and then swept away by romanticism and passion. The premarital period is to assess carefully, both emotionally and rationally, whether you can successfully share your lives as a married couple. It is impossible to engage in this process without discussing negative feelings and difficult issues. The man who tells his friends, "She's absolutely perfect, we agree on everything," is kidding himself and in a paradoxical way is not being fair to the woman. People do not belong on pedestals. When she fails it is a particularly hard fall. Having to be perfect robs a woman of her individuality, and she becomes merely a reflection of his imagined ideal.

The question about negative feelings is not whether they'll occur, but how to deal with and express them in a nondestructive manner. The primary function of negative feelings is to signal a problem that needs to be addressed. Whether the feeling is hurt, frustration, anxiety, loneliness, envy, depression, anger, or boredom, it is a signal about you, your partner, the relationship, and/or situation. Attend to the feeling rather than deny it. There is great pressure to be swept away by the intensity of romantic love and to deny negative feelings. This needs to be resisted. Relationships get into trouble when you pretend everything is perfect, deny negative feelings, and avoid difficult issues.

Being aware of a feeling and choosing how to express it are different dimensions. When Barry was studying to be a psychologist in the late 1960s, there was a strong movement toward "getting in touch with feelings" and "expressing feelings in the here and now." These approaches sounded good and were promoted by couples encounter groups. However, empirical research did not confirm their efficacy.

The value of being aware of feelings is universally accepted. How to express feelings appropriately is filled with controversy and opposing advice. We believe that the expression of feelings—as much of human behavior—is on a continuum. Expression at either extreme is likely to cause problems for a couple, especially a new one. Couples who are afraid of expressing feelings run the risk of the relationship stagnating and becoming increasingly frustrating. Men often have difficulty expressing sadness, weakness, ambivalence, or depression; women have trouble with anger, assertiveness, and needs for autonomy. People who cannot express emotions run the risk of having role-governed relationships that negate individuality and couple creativity. On the other extreme, people who are emotionally labile, who go from joy to tears in a matter of minutes or who express each emotion intensely as they become aware of it, are likely to have volatile and unstable relationships.

Emotional expression needs to be congruent with thoughts, attitudes, and values, and understood in the context of the couple's relationship. Feeling angry does not give you the right to abuse someone. Feeling lonely or depressed is an important signal, but desperately wanting your spouse to rescue you is self-defeating. Mild irritation needs to be expressed differently from rage. The person who is frequently depressed or rageful is shunned. Legitimate desires are not taken seriously because they are lost in the intense communication.

How did you experience and express negative feelings when you began as a couple? One of the most common fights married couples have is about feeling deceived—in the courting period the partner pretended something didn't matter when, in truth, he felt hurt or depressed. The courtship period is the right time to discuss and express these feelings and work toward understanding and resolution.

EVERYDAY HASSLES AND MAJOR ISSUES

Couples confront a myriad of difficulties. These may be divided into two areas, everyday hassles and major issues. Couples and marital theorists believe that major issues stress a marriage most, but research shows that everyday hassles tear at the marital fabric. Examples of major issues are decisions about moving or about whether an aging parent should live with you, one spouse having an affair, the prospect of bankruptcy, incidents of violence. Everyday hassles include not vacuuming as promised, lack of affection, losing the car keys, ignoring birthdays, forgetting to balance the checkbook, petting the dog before kissing the spouse, being a couch potato watching whatever is on TV, not expressing feelings, one person always stuck driving the kids' car pool.

Both major issues and everyday hassles need to be addressed. We strongly believe in the importance of couple agreements to deal with these issues. Self-esteem and the marital bond are promoted by viable couple agreements.

EVERYDAY HASSLES

The place to start is with everyday hassles. A characteristic of successful, stable marriages is they are based on a positive influence process. You state feelings, make requests, and your spouse responds in a respectful, caring manner. Discuss alternatives and reach an agreement that addresses the problem and meets individual and couple needs. Making agreements to deal with everyday hassles sounds simple, but is difficult and complex in application to real-life couple problems. When you've made two or three agreements and see that they work, your belief in the positive influence process is reinforced, as is the value of making couple agreements, and your marital bond.

Everyday hassles cause irritation and frustration that devitalizes the couple bond. You cannot completely do away with hassles, but can alleviate the most common ones. To cite an example, Barry dramatically reduced his habit of spitting on the sidewalk when Emily said she found it disgusting and that it interfered with enjoyment of their walks. Emily stopped teasing Barry about behavior from his past when he told her this hurt his feelings. In themselves these agreements might not seem like much, but they were significant because they demonstrated that we listened respectfully and influenced each other. An agreement does not have to be perfect, but it does have to be honored by both spouses and make a significant change.

Exercise One: Changing Everyday Hassles

Each person writes three habits she would like the spouse to change. Be clear and specific in identifying the request: "Before you come to bed, I would like you to brush your teeth," "Keep the checkbook balanced on a weekly basis," "Put down the lid after you use the toilet," "Give me fifteen minutes to be alone and decompress before starting house projects," "When you take the children, assume responsibility for them, don't expect me to get them ready." "Call your parents without my reminding you," "Bring fruit and coffee on weekend mornings," "Don't tell more than three stories at a party." The spouse considers these requests and agrees to the one he feels would be in his best interest and could be successfully implemented. He commits to the new behavior and tells her what she can do to help. Successfully implementing change requires motivation, assuming personal responsibility, a method to implement the change and monitor progress, and support and encouragement from the spouse. Change is an incremental process, not an all-or-nothing overnight miracle. Changing habits is not easy, but is achievable if the person remains committed to the goal and does not become distracted or discouraged. Problem-solving is the adaptive response to setbacks so that the process stays on track. Two traps that interfere with change are setting perfectionistic, unrealistic goals, and attacking the spouse rather than working together to change the problem.

Once you have agreed on a behavior change, give the spouse time to focus on and implement it. Don't make one spouse's behavior contingent on the other. If one spouse has agreed to stop smoking in the house and the other has agreed to vacuum on weekends, and the spouse is having difficulty with the vacuuming, it does not mean the other can smoke in the house. This is not a tit-for-tat game. The person agrees to change because it is in his best interest and will promote the relationship. It is his agreement and his commitment.

When you've had success with two or three agreements for changing everyday hassles, you can make more ambitious agreements to modify major problems. With the reduction in everyday hassles, you'll have more energy to enjoy your life and marriage.

Nora and Nelson. Nora loved being married and having five children. However, she was becoming increasingly drained and exhausted in dealing with Nelson, a government manager. Nelson had attended classes on interpersonal relations and supervision, and felt he understood people better than Nora. She was a commercial leasing agent, a career requiring hard selling in a very competitive market. They regularly argued over whose view of human nature was correct. With five children, two careers, a large extended family living in the area, and a good deal of social and athletic involvement emanating from their children's activities, Nora and Nelson had a full life, everyday hassles, and two major problem areas.

The most disruptive hassles revolved around conflicts in arranging the children's activities, especially responsibility for car pools, and disagreements concerning music the children listened to and their hairstyles. The two major problems were how to make financial decisions and Nora's desire to move to a larger house in a better neighborhood. This couple provided a good example of how unsatisfactory compromises lead to continued frustration. Nelson would say, "We have to compromise," and he seemed so rational and reasonable that Nora went along even though instinct told her that this would not work (and it didn't). It was not until they discussed hard alternatives and solutions that entailed significant changes that they broke the impasse. Splitting car pools fifty-fifty and being scrupulously even with each child's activities simply didn't work. The truth was that Nelson could tolerate, and actually enjoyed, car pools. Nora agreed to take the one car pool he couldn't stand. They bought a large plywood divider for the kitchen and each Sunday all extracurricular activities, with car pool assignments, were put on the board.

Nelson was a rocker in the sixties who enjoyed oldies music, but accepted his kids' brand of rock. While in college he had long hair, although when the children looked at old pictures of their father, they found it inconceivable that this short-haired, clean-shaven, government-manager-father was the same person. Nelson loved to entertain his children and their friends with sixties stories. Nora was a lover of classical music and wanted her children to look and act appropriately, and not be a source of embarrassment reflecting badly on the parents. They had tried a number of systems including taking turns on what music to listen to and going for monthly haircuts, none of which worked satisfactorily. For the music controversy, technology provided an acceptable answer. The driver chose what he wanted on the car radio. Others brought their Walkmans with headsets and listened to their music. This agreement worked well.

Hair is one of those adult-child struggles that is much ado about nothing. Nora reluctantly agreed that the adolescent's hair was not a symbol of the kind of person he was. School and community projects, a good relationship with his grandparents, and refraining from drug activity were rightly judged as of greater importance. Not all agreements can meet individual needs and successfully resolve an issue. Nelson and Nora had to accept that there was no good solution on adolescent hair.

Finances are one of the most difficult, complex issues couples face. Nelson came from a traditional family where the man made more money and had veto over family spending. It was not a good system, but everyone understood the rules. Nelson remembered thinking his father was irrational and dictatorial about money, and felt sorry for his mother, who had to put up with that nonsense. Nora did not like the way her parents handled money. Her father worried too much and her mother had little sense of financial matters.

In their first years of marriage, Nora and Nelson were having babies and saving for a "starter" house. As with other couples of their generation, they received parental help with a down payment and were able to obtain a house at a reasonable price. With five children it was nearly impossible to meet bills on Nelson's government salary, so Nora worked part time selling residential real estate. She enjoyed the field, and after a year switched to commercial leasing. Within four years, Nora's salary exceeded Nelson's. The wife earning more than the husband is becoming more of a pattern in our culture. Nelson said he loved the idea of his wife earning a substantial income, but it raised difficult issues and caused unanticipated problems. He began to doubt the value of his work, even though previously he had felt competent and enjoyed being a manager. This coincided with a decade of "bureaucrat bashing," which lowered morale among public employees and intensified his sense of being undervalued. To succeed in commercial leasing, Nora needed to be aggressive and self-assured. That is an appropriate professional role, but it is not healthy to transfer those attributes to the more complex, emotional domain of marital and family relationships. Nora both envied and resented male colleagues who seemed oblivious to career-family conflicts. One year Nora received a $14,000 bonus, the second largest in her division. Rather than bragging about it, she worried how it would affect Nelson since that meant she would earn $20,000 more than he.

In traditional marriages, money equaled power. Since the man made more money he had more power. Does this mean that when the woman makes more money she assumes decision-making and veto power? Although this might work in certain marriages, it was not acceptable to Nelson nor did Nora desire to wield financial power. She did want her contributions acknowledged and discretion to spend money to make life easier, such as having a twice-a-week cleaning service.

The most difficult point of contention was buying a bigger house in a nicer neighborhood. Four children ranging in age from nine to seventeen were living at home. The oldest daughter was away at college. Nelson argued that their present house had served the family well, that the kids enjoyed the neighborhood and their schools, and the need for a bigger house was decreasing, not increasing. It is paradoxical that as some people begin to earn more money and can afford a bigger house, their children are leaving home so the need is less. Nora wanted a larger house with more bathrooms, a family room for the children, and a room for a home office/hobby area. As a real estate professional, she believed that moving to a better neighborhood would be a good financial investment.

Money and house decisions are more a matter of what kind of life a family desires than a financial investment. Nelson and Nora discussed the issue with the children and listened to their feelings, but as this was an adult decision, the children did not have a vote.

When we describe how a couple talk about issues, discuss alternatives, and come to an agreement it sounds cut and dried. The reality for Nora and Nelson was that it was a complex, time-consuming, confusing, and emotionally draining process with all manner of conflicts and missteps. They looked at houses with a real estate agent, discussed the decision with couple friends and people at work, read articles and books on home mortgages and money management, and spent hours sitting at the kitchen table going over pros and cons. They decided to stay in their present house and build a four-room addition. Through the chaos of construction, they second-guessed the decision a hundred times. Between construction workers, dust, and moving children and furniture, it was a chaotic time. Ultimately, they felt they had made the right choice. In every decision there is a cost-benefit tradeoff. Personal desires and emotional concerns are more important than financial or investment factors.

House issues reach a decision point and are resolved. This is not so with money issues which are dealt with—or not—on an ongoing basis. There are many possible money management systems, the most common being a system of "ours, yours, mine," or putting all money in a common fund with an agreement that any expenditure over a certain amount, $200 perhaps, must be agreed to by both spouses. The agreement Nora and Nelson developed was that they contributed an equal amount to the common fund. Each took $150 per month that didn't have to be accounted for, and everything else went into the ''our'' budget. Nora's additional salary and bonuses went toward a house improvement, kids' college, and retirement fund. This agreement allowed them to better accept the salary discrepancy. Nelson was relieved that Nora would not use money as a club over him.

On TV shows and in magazine articles there are perfect solutions and the couple live happily ever after. Real-life couples find that few agreements are perfect, but that making agreements works. The couple are better able to discuss feelings, develop alternatives, deal with everyday hassles, and continue working on resolving hard issues. Marriage is an ongoing process. Nora and Nelson realized that if they were to maintain marital satisfaction, they would need to discuss negative feelings and deal with difficult issues as they arose.

Exercise Two: Agreements About Major Issues

Every marriage has difficult issues, some transitory and others ongoing. Some are relatively straightforward, others are extremely complex both emotionally and practically.

In this exercise, each person lists two to five major issues facing the couple. Examples include arranging nursing home care for an aging parent, choosing an educational and tutorial program for a learning-disabled child, handling a phobia or depression, one spouse's career dissatisfaction, developing a new money management system, a blended family situation in which ex-in-laws want more involvement with their grandchildren, one person attending a twelve-step self-help program and the spouse resenting the time commitment and intrusion on her life, conflict over religious practices, one spouse feeling unfairly burdened by house and/or parenting responsibilities, a difficult stepparent/stepchild relationship, an eating or smoking problem, rebuilding trust and intimacy after discovery of an extramarital affair, uncertainty over job security, lack of couple friends, one spouse deciding to return to school and needing to work out financial and practical arrangements, dealing with childhood physical and/or sexual abuse, dissatisfaction with house or community, lack of time to pursue personal or recreational activities. After creating your list of issues, share it with your spouse and choose one area you both agree is problematic.

The problem-solving agreement process is not easy, but it is vital. Good agreements increase self-esteem and strengthen the marital bond.

The steps in the process:

1. Define a major issue you are motivated to address. Choose a problem where there is a reasonable chance to make significant improvement.
2. Each discusses feelings and perceptions. The spouse listens in a respectful, caring manner.
3. Generate alternatives that address the issue. Brainstorm a range of alternatives. Then do a cost-benefit assessment for each alternative.
4. Negotiate an agreement that addresses each spouse's concerns, is clear, and has a good chance of resolving the issue. Optimally, the agreement would meet the needs of each individual and strengthen the couple bond. At a minimum, each can live with the agreement. Don't agree to something that is not in your best interest or does not have a good chance of succeeding.
5. Decide how to put the agreement into effect and monitor progress to maximize the likelihood of a successful outcome. Implementation, the most neglected phase, requires both people being committed to the positive influence process. If there are glitches, redefine and problem solve until the agreement works.

Go through these steps in a thoughtful, careful manner. For the first two agreements, be sure you work through each step so you learn the skills and develop worthwhile agreements. This might sound easy, but in reality making agreements is a complex and emotionally taxing process. Be sure you are satisfied with each step in the process rather than rushing to completion. When you reach an impasse, don't avoid the issues or allow the process to degenerate into a power struggle. Continue to work as a cooperative, respectful team. This is at the heart of being able to reach an agreement. Share feelings and desires, listen in a respectful and caring manner, discuss alternatives, reach an agreement, and implement it successfully. This process will enhance self-esteem and strengthen the marital bond.

ISSUES THAT CANNOT BE SUCCESSFULLY RESOLVED

In many self-help articles and books there is an implicit (and sometimes explicit) promise that with enough communication, commitment, therapy, prayer, uncovering of childhood trauma, etc., any and all problems can be successfully resolved. This is a self-defeating and unrealistic expectation. We believe in the serenity prayer, "Give me the courage to change what is changeable, the ability to accept what I can't change, and the wisdom to know the difference." There are some issues that cannot be successfully resolved. There are no perfect people, perfect lives, or perfect marriages. Part of the human condition is accepting that there are issues and problems that will continue to vex you, but need not control self-esteem and marriage.

In our lives, the everyday hassles of Barry's inability to type and Emily's inability to manage finances are chronic sources of frustration, but are accepted as realities. Major issues include regret that we could not help our parents achieve happier lives and marriages, but we realize that adult children are usually not able to alter the lives of their parents despite knowledge, skill, or good intentions. An ongoing issue is that Emily loves small-town living with an emphasis on antiques, history, remodeling our home, and gardening. Barry appreciates those things, but values travel, the diversity of a large city, theater, and ethnic restaurants. We recognize our separateness and individuality, and strive to make agreements that balance individual and couple needs. The balance is not easy to maintain, but is vital in strengthening self-esteem and ensuring an intimate, stable marriage. Dealing with difficult issues rather than avoiding them is crucial.

THE DIFFERENCE BETWEEN ACCEPTING PROBLEMS AND SACRIFICING SELF-ESTEEM

Not only are there problems that defy solution, but in every marriage there may be weeks, or even years, when problems interfere with well-being and marital happiness. How can you differentiate between problems that need to be accepted and problems that sabotage a marriage? The key is the effect on self-esteem. For instance, an unsatisfactory job and money problems are difficult, but need not control your life or sabotage the marriage. However, feeling guilty and resentful because your spouse forces you to stay at the job and belittles your lack of competence is destructive for self-esteem and calls into question the viability of the marriage. Caring for a terminally ill parent can be personally stressful and disruptive to the marital bond, but you support each other during this difficult time. Contrast that with the couple who argued constantly over whose family was "crazier." A central component in an intimate marriage is trusting and being vulnerable. Vulnerable disclosures turned against you lower self-esteem, damage the trust bond, and threaten the marriage.

How does the spouse react to your psychological distress? If you are arrested for not paying a speeding ticket or a friend is angry with you, does your spouse offer emotional support or does he say, "I told you so"? It is important to confront self-defeating behavior such as not paying a ticket, but only in the context of emotional support. The spouse can help you deal with difficult issues such as depression, phobias, obsessive-compulsive behavior, failures at work, lack of a degree which blocks a promotion, personality conflict with a supervisor, emotional distance from a child, a difficult in-law relationship. Confrontation is more likely to be successful when it is in the context of a caring, supportive relationship. Confrontation can build self-esteem when it addresses something you denied or minimized. You will feel better if the issue is discussed, even if it cannot be resolved.

Chronic problems are particularly burdensome. You muster psychological energy to deal with an acute weight problem or erectile dysfunction. When it's your eighth diet or the erection problem is in its sixth year and is compounded by inhibited sexual desire, finding the motivation to try again to deal with it is difficult. Yet if chronic problems are neglected, they become more severe and a bigger drain on self-esteem and the marital bond. Being twenty pounds overweight is problematic but allowing it to become fifty pounds is medically, psychologically, and maritally a potential disaster. Marriages can and do survive sexual dysfunction, but if the couple totally stops being sexual, especially if this includes stopping affection, it devastates the intimate bond.

Chronic problems must be addressed; otherwise they become dominant. Barry's clinical practice is filled with individuals and couples who are angry at themselves and each other because they have to confront a difficult problem. They complain that this is unjust, why won't it just go away. They squander time and energy engaging in "what if" thinking. This is part of the denial process, of refusing to deal with a difficult, chronic problem. In a respectful, caring, but confrontative matter, Barry encourages them to step up to the problem. He cannot guarantee a successful resolution, but if the problem is not addressed it will become more draining and severe. Chronic problems subvert self-esteem and the marital bond. If you deal with the problem, it will not control you even if it does not result in a satisfactory resolution.

CLOSING THOUGHTS

This was one of the most difficult chapters to write, and probably anxiety-provoking to read. We would love to live in a childlike, fairy tale world where love is enough and communication resolves all problems. Life and marriage is simply not that way. We purposely put this chapter in the enhancement section because a sign of a good marriage is the ability to deal with negative feelings and difficult issues. One value of marriage is realizing that you are not alone, that you have an intimate friend who is supportive through sad or difficult times.

We do not believe the old adage that dealing with adversity is good for you. We urge couples to deal with difficult issues because unless they are addressed, self-esteem and the marital bond deteriorate. Knowing you can disclose negative feelings and have your spouse's support in confronting difficult and painful issues bolsters self-esteem and the marital bond.

SEVEN

Sexuality: Energizing the Intimate Bond

The major functions of sexuality are a shared pleasure, a means of creating and reinforcing intimacy, and a tension reducer to deal with the frustrations and hassles of everyday life and marriage. Sexuality is a positive, integral part of marriage. When sexuality is healthy it's a relatively minor part (fifteen to twenty percent), with its main function to energize the marital bond. Sexual dysfunction or dissatisfaction can be a serious drain on self-esteem and the marriage. Sexual problems are a major reason for divorce.

You are a sexual person from the day you're born to the day you die. You deserve the positive role that sexuality plays in self-esteem and marriage. Sexuality is more than genitals, intercourse, and orgasm: it is a natural, integral part of who you are as a person. The essence of sexuality is giving and receiving pleasurable touching. Our prescription for satisfying sex is an intimate relationship, nondemand pleasuring, and multiple stimulation.

Barry tires of hearing couples recall how passionate and frequent their premarital sex was and how disappointing marital sex is. Upon closer examination, they discover that it was not the quality but the illicitness, newness, and romanticism of their premarital experiences, and their desire to win over the prospective spouse. Once married, sex lost its pizazz and lapsed into an uninspired routine that declined in frequency and satisfaction. The initial charge of romantic love is fragile and short-lived.

It takes most people at least six months to create a quality couple sexual style. This means developing pleasure-oriented touching and sexual scenarios that promote desire, arousal, orgasm, and satisfaction. Touching can occur both inside and outside the bedroom, and be nondemanding, that is, not intended to culminate in intercourse and orgasm.

The key to sexual desire is openness to and anticipation of a sexual encounter. Each person feels free to initiate affectionate and sensual touching as well as intercourse. Arousal involves receptivity and responsivity to sexual stimulation. Subjective arousal usually precedes objective arousal. In other words, feeling responsive occurs before erection and vaginal lubrication.

Orgasm is not the ultimate measure of satisfaction. Orgasm lasts a few seconds and subjectively is similar for females and males. Physiologically, orgasm involves a series of pelvic contractions, and for males is accompanied by ejaculation. Typically, the male will have one orgasm, which occurs during intercourse. Female orgasm is more complex and variable, but not better or worse. A woman might be nonorgasmic, singly orgasmic, or multiorgasmic, either during the pleasuring/foreplay period, during intercourse, or in afterplay. Psychologically, orgasm involves letting go and is the natural result of high arousal. Magazines and books discuss vaginal versus clitoral orgasm, G-spot orgasm, extended orgasm, etc. This is great for book sales, talk shows, and bar talk, but scientifically it's nonsense. Physiologically, the same orgasmic process occurs regardless of whether the type of stimulation is masturbation, intercourse, manual, or oral stimulation.

Emotional satisfaction is the most important element of sexual response, but the least understood. Ideally, sexuality would serve as an energizing and bonding experience. As with any complex human activity, there is variability in sexual expression and satisfaction. Couples who expect each experience to be great have unrealistic expectations and are setting themselves up for disappointment. Well-functioning couples report that in approximately forty percent of sexual interactions there is equal desire, arousal, orgasm, and satisfaction. Fifteen to twenty percent of interactions one spouse finds very satisfying while the other enjoys the experience. In another fifteen to twenty percent one spouse finds the experience satisfying and the other is glad it happened but didn't find it particularly fulfilling. In another ten to fifteen percent one person finds the sex fulfills a need while the spouse goes along for the ride. In five to ten percent of occasions these well-functioning couples find the sex is either mediocre or a downright failure. Couples who are able to laugh or shrug off mediocre or negative experiences have a coping attitude that facilitates accepting sexual variability without disrupting couple intimacy.

It is important to be realistic about intercourse frequency. Most couples believe others are more sexually active. The average range of intercourse frequency is four times a week to once every two weeks. Typical intercourse frequency is one to three times per week. Sex is not a matter of quantity and performance. The idea is not to keep up with the Joneses, but to develop a couple style that emphasizes comfort, pleasure, and intimacy.

SEXUAL PROBLEMS AND REALISTIC EXPECTATIONS

Almost all couples experience sexual dissatisfaction or dysfunction on an occasional basis. Whether it is the male who ejaculates early or does not maintain an erection sufficient for intercourse or the woman who finds herself unable to become aroused or is nonorgasmic, it is normal to not function perfectly at each sexual opportunity. Books and articles would have us believe everyone is experiencing the most exquisitely satisfying sex in the history of the world. In reality, rates of sexual dysfunction and dissatisfaction have changed little in the past twenty years. The type of sexual problems have shifted from those caused by lack of information and awareness to those caused by unrealistic expectations and performance anxiety.

Couples with sexual difficulties, especially chronic dysfunction, find it burdensome. The male with an erection problem labels himself impotent, and that becomes his personal, as well as sexual, self-definition. The woman who has never experienced orgasm during couple sex mislabels herself frigid and feels she is less of a woman. Sexuality enhances an intimate relationship. When there is dysfunction, the problem becomes predominant and drains the relationship of vitality and intimacy. Sexuality would ideally constitute fifteen to twenty percent of individual self-esteem and the marital bond. Sexual dysfunction can sabotage self-confidence, feel like seventy-five percent of self-esteem, and have an inordinately negative effect on the marriage.

Sarah and Hank. After the initial glow, most couples do not create a high quality sexual relationship. Sarah was twenty-nine when she met Hank, who was exactly three weeks younger (he teased her unmercifully about being the older woman who seduced the younger man). Sarah was more sexually experienced, although Hank was more interested in being married.

By twenty-nine, Sarah was disappointed in males and sex. Since high school she had worked to improve relationships, trying to understand what a man wanted. In college she took courses and read self-help books on how to seduce a man into being more intimate, why women love too much and make poor choices, how to fight fair, how to keep your man monogamous. The pressure and responsibility was on the woman, which was unfair and unrealistic. Responsibility for contraception and prevention of sexually transmitted diseases was primarily, and often solely, the woman's concern. She supported friends through abortions while the male kept his distance. Sarah was an excellent user of contraceptives, having tried the diaphragm but preferring the birth control pill. She saw herself as a liberated woman, comfortable with sexuality. However, she found it tiring to work at relationships that ultimately ended and was frustrated with the singles scene.

Hank's experience with dating and sexuality was different; it hadn't been a big deal. In college he had been serious and hard-working. He enjoyed stories and jokes about crazy parties more than the parties themselves. He was shy, but clear about the kind of woman he liked. His relationships lasted at least a year. Sex was functional, but not passionate. Hank valued settling down and getting married, and was surprised he was single at twenty-nine. He had moved a great deal for his career and had not found a woman he felt would grow with him.

Hank met Sarah during Sunday brunch at a friend's house. He was attracted to Sarah's large, hazel eyes and the size and shape of her breasts. Hank was a very visually oriented man and this maintained his sexual desire throughout the marriage. Sarah enjoyed talking with Hank about current events. After brunch he invited her for a bike ride, which Sarah found was a pleasant way for them to get to know each other. She was pleased that he didn't come on strong. Hank was affectionate and had a nice touch. Sarah enjoyed being in a relationship in which she didn't have to work so hard.

The passion that comes with romantic love is an experience to be savored. Twenty years later Sarah and Hank fondly recall the time they stayed in bed for thirty-six hours, made love on a blanket under the boardwalk, kissed and touched in the car and were so aroused they made love in the hallway. It was an exciting and passionate time. However, compared to the quality of their present lovemaking, they'd come a long way. Newness and illicitness carried sexuality and they wouldn't have had it any other way. It was not until they were married eight months that Hank and Sarah began to talk and experiment with pleasuring techniques and sexual scenarios.

The sexual turning point came when Sarah told Hank that she needed slower, more prolonged touching, and found his constant sexual talk offensive. Hank had heard from male friends that the way to turn a woman on was to whisper sexual fantasies in her ear right before intercourse. Hank had done this in other relationships, and considered himself a sophisticated lover. Initially Sarah found sexually explicit talk cute and intriguing, although not erotic. Over time, especially since he always did it, it became irritating. She did not want to hurt his feelings or insult him, but did want a change. Any sexual technique done every time will become mechanical and routine. Sarah desired greater emotional connection and asked Hank to express his feelings instead of his fantasies. She was especially responsive to long, slow, tender touching. Like many women, Sarah's preference was nongenital, sensual touching to get her in the mood before she could be responsive to breast and vulva stimulation. She enjoyed a variety of sexual scenarios instead of settling into one or two predictable formats. She enjoyed "nooners," a pattern that served them well when they had children—they would be sexual and then nap during the children's naps. Sarah's sexual self-esteem increased as they communicated feelings and preferences and improved the quality of lovemaking. She trusted that she could make requests and Hank would be receptive.

The sexual breakthrough for Hank occurred nine years later, a few months before their tenth wedding anniversary. Hank had complained that Sarah didn't initiate sex. One evening she initiated right after he put the kids to sleep. Hank pretended to be interested, but was distracted by financial worries. He was somewhat aroused, but lost his erection right before intromission. He made a desperate attempt to gain entry, but with lowered arousal and growing panic, sex was a fiasco. He blamed Sarah, which confused and annoyed her. She felt that Hank had given her a mixed message about initiation.

The next few intercourses, mechanical and low quality, were at Hank's initiation. As soon as he got an erection, he moved to intercourse. It was as if Sarah's feelings and sexual response were unimportant. Three weeks later, during intercourse, Hank's penis slipped out of Sarah's vagina. After two desperate tries, he gave up and turned away from her. Sarah lay there a few minutes, deciding what to do. She did not feel that Hank blamed her, which allowed her to think clearly about what happened. Hank was experiencing performance anxiety. Sex was no longer fun, but had become an intercourse performance. Rather than being passive or having an unproductive what-went-wrong talk, Sarah chose to pleasure Hank. She began by rubbing his back and tickling his chest, but when Hank began to get hard again, rather than "jumping on the erection" to see if they could have intercourse, Sarah told him to lie back, that she wanted to give to him. As she manually and orally stimulated Hank, he ejaculated. Sarah enjoyed knowing she could arouse him, and they had a warm, intimate time before drifting off to sleep.

The next morning Hank suggested they take a walk. He told Sarah how much he appreciated her understanding and sexual giving. He was aware that he was falling into the performance anxiety trap. He'd taken erections and intercourse for granted and at thirty-nine years old he could no longer do that. He needed Sarah to be his active, involved sexual friend. Both realized quality sexuality was more than genitals, intercourse, and orgasm. Sarah found it easier to be aroused and orgasmic with manual and oral stimulation, although she enjoyed intercourse and occasionally was orgasmic during intercourse.

Sarah had read articles about sexuality in feminist magazines and was aware that men and women in their thirties, forties, and fifties had to adopt a broader-based view of sexuality. The experience was better when there was more sexual give and take and emotional connection. "Pleasuring" was what it was all about. Pleasuring was more than foreplay to get them ready for intercourse. Sarah enjoyed nongenital pleasuring, followed by oral breast stimulation and manual clitoral stimulation before intercourse. Hank enjoyed receiving genital stimulation while he was pleasuring Sarah and was especially aroused by fellatio before beginning intercourse. They agreed that Sarah would guide his penis into her vagina.

Once Sarah and Hank learned to talk, touch, and play, they made a comfortable transition from automatic, autonomous erections to a mutual, interactive sexual scenario. Learning this inoculated them against sexual problems as they aged.

Sarah and Hank felt more like lovers than when they first married. They developed quality pleasuring and sexual scenarios, realizing that sex was more than intercourse. They had no intention of resting on their laurels. They devoted time and energy to sexual intimacy. Intimacy is not achieved by trying to change your partner. Intimacy involves being aware of your comfort, feelings, and needs. Share these, make requests instead of demands. Sexual intimacy includes nondemand pleasuring, multiple stimulation, emotional sharing, and being an intimate team.

Exercise: Nondemand Pleasuring

From experiences as a couple and Barry's work with sexual dysfunction, we are convinced that the essence of sexuality is giving and receiving pleasurable touching. This exercise allows you to discover if that is true for you. When couples have completed sex therapy, this exercise is suggested as something they do every six weeks or two months to keep in touch with sensuality. Some couples modify the exercise and utilize genital touching; others keep the prohibition on intercourse but allow themselves to be orgasmic with manual, oral, or rubbing stimulation. Our suggestion is to focus on sensuality, refraining from genital stimulation and orgasm. The focus is on giving and receiving pleasurable, sensual touching. Many couples are comfortable with clothes-on affection such as hand-holding, kissing, or hugging, but avoid sensual experiences. Sensuality involves being nude or semiclothed, engaging in whole body stroking, caressing, and nondemand touching.

Set aside forty-five minutes to an hour and a half. Put the answering machine on or take the phone off the hook. Be sure the kids are out or asleep. Lock the door so you're not distracted or interrupted. In our culture, it is typically the male's role to initiate. Ideally, both spouses should feel free to initiate. To reinforce this, have the woman initiate the pleasuring exercise.

Begin by sitting and talking for five or ten minutes over a cup of coffee or glass of wine. Share an experience when you felt particularly intimate. Touching facilitates feelings of emotional closeness. Ask your spouse to put his hands out and explore his hands and fingers. Notice the differences in size and texture. What would it be like if this were the last time you were to touch his hands? Caress each hand in a tender and caring manner.

Take a shower or bath together. The focus isn't on cleanliness, but being comfortable with nudity and increasing awareness of sensual stimuli. Try a different soap, a bubble bath, or experiment with temperatures or types of spray. Soap his back, caressing it as you do. Trace the muscles and contours, gently rub and massage. Soap his front and touch the hollows of his neck and the soft area below the ribs. Soap genitals, hips, and legs. Then let him soap you.

Dry each other, taking your time. Give your partner the benefit of a slow, tender approach. Look at your spouse as if this was the first time you'd seen him. Notice one or two things about his body you find particularly attractive. Slide his arms around your waist; enjoy the warmth and closeness.

Go to the bedroom nude or put a towel or robe on and leave it at the door. Pleasuring is best done in the nude. Be sure the room is at a comfortable temperature and there is enough light to see your partner's body. Some couples enjoy doing this by candlelight, and use scented candles to offer additional sensual stimuli. Put on your favorite music to add to the ambiance.

The male has three tasks. The first is to allow himself to

be passive and receive pleasure. The second is to keep his eyes closed so he can concentrate on feelings (and she is less self-conscious). His third task is to be aware of what parts of his body and types of touch are sensuous.

The woman can feel comfortable giving a wide variety of touch. Touch for yourself rather than trying to second guess what he wants. Look at and stroke from the top of his head to the bottom of his feet. Talk can be distracting; focus on communicating through touch.

Massage his shoulders gently—this is not a vigorous back rub. Rub tenderly using your entire hand; move slowly down the back and sides. Allow the touching to be gentle and rhythmic, avoid sudden movements. Be aware of appealing characteristics that you might not have noticed—freckles, tiny scars, muscle indentations. When you reach the waist, place your thumbs together, spread your fingers, and gently press and knead as you caress his sides and lower back.

The giver provides a variety of touching experiences so the receiver can increase awareness of sensuality and pleasure. Feel free to innovate. Be spontaneous. These are guidelines, not rules.

Hold and caress his feet. Notice the length of his toes, the texture of the nails. Place your palm so it covers the arch, and curl your fingers over the top of his foot. Notice the heel as you rub it with the palm of your hand.

Once you've explored the back of his body, slowly roll him over and start on the front. Explore and caress his face. Remind him to close his eyes. You might kiss his closed eyelids. Gently caress away the lines from his forehead. Stroke his face and be aware of at least one feature that you enjoy looking at and touching. Give a scalp massage or gently run your fingers through his hair. Slowly and tenderly stroke his chest. Tickle his chest hairs or play with his nipples; many men enjoy this. Rub your hands around his stomach and ribs. Feel free to look at his penis and testicles, but don't touch. He may or may not have an erection. Women tend to view a man's erection as pressure or a demand rather than seeing it as a compliment, a natural response to pleasure. Enjoy his penis for what it is, a special part of him. Let the exploration and touching proceed to his inner thighs, legs, feet, and toes.

When you've completed the nondemand sensuous exploration, switch roles and let him be the giver. Although most couples switch roles during the exercise, some prefer to have a separate session where the roles are reversed. In an intimate relationship both people can be comfortable giving and receiving. Interestingly, many males find it harder to receive than to give.

The male needn't try to emulate her approach; he can touch in ways he enjoys. Focus on exploring, being comfortable, and sharing sensuality. The key is slow, tender, rhythmic, and caring touching. Enjoy giving in a nongenital, nondemanding way. Traditionally, when the man strokes a woman his goal is to "turn her on" and prove he is a good lover. There's no need for either person to prove anything. The woman focuses on the kinds of touch and parts of her body that feel sensuous. The man can enjoy touching for himself and sharing pleasure.

After this exercise, or the next day, sit over a cup of coffee or a drink and discuss the experience. Share positive feelings and perceptions first and then discuss negatives with a request for change. What did you learn about initiating and sensuality that can be incorporated into lovemaking? How can you integrate sensuality with sexuality and intercourse?

SEXUAL FUNCTION AND DYSFUNCTION

Sexual functioning means that each spouse is capable of desire, arousal, orgasm, and emotional satisfaction. Does this mean that if each time you have sex you or your spouse don't experience desire, arousal, orgasm, and feel satisfied that you have a sexual problem? Absolutely not! This illustrates the importance of establishing realistic expectations. Even the happiest and most sexually functional couples find five to ten percent of their sexual interactions to be mediocre or downright bombs. In the middle of a sexual experience one of us, usually Barry, will ask whether the other is into it. Emily might say, "I'm going along for the ride, I thought you were feeling sexy." We can laugh or shrug this off and agree to be sexual later that day or the next, when we're feeling more rested, involved, or sexier. These experiences are not a threat to sexual self-esteem or the intimate bond. There are times when one spouse is not desirous, arousal is lost and not regained, orgasm is not reached, or the experience is not satisfying. This reflects normal sexual variability. In sports, no one wins all the games. If you win two of three you'll be a champion. Sex is a cooperative team sport, not a win-lose competition. Sexuality nurtures and energizes the marital bond. If sexuality lowers self-esteem or devitalizes the marital bond, there is a problem that needs to be addressed.

FREQUENCY AND TYPES OF SEXUAL DYSFUNCTION

Approximately fifty percent of married couples (and sixty-five percent of unmarried individuals) experience a sexual dissatisfaction or dysfunction. Every relationship has at least one experience where sex is unsatisfactory, a "bomb." Human beings are not perfect machines, but people, whose sexual experiences are complex and variable. A sexual difficulty is not considered a dysfunction unless it has existed for over six months. Unfortunately, most people allow sexual problems to fester for years. When they consult a therapist, they have to address not only the dysfunction, but the layers of confusion, frustration, blaming, and anger that have built. Sexual problems do not remain stable, but become burdensome and chronic.

For women, these are the most common sexual complaints:

1. Nonorgasmic response during intercourse.
2. Inhibited sexual desire.
3. Secondary nonorgasmic response.
4. Painful intercourse.

5. Primary nonorgasmic response.
6. Vaginismus.

The distinction between primary and secondary dysfunction is that primary means sexual functioning has always been problematic; secondary means there is a history of good sexual functioning. For example, primary nonorgasmic response with a partner means that the woman has never been orgasmic during partner sex, although she has been orgasmic through masturbation; secondary nonorgasmic means she has been orgasmic, but is not at present.

NON-ORGASMIC RESPONSE

The most frequent female sexual complaint, not being orgasmic during intercourse, is *not* a sexual dysfunction. It is the male who insists the woman perform like he does and have one orgasm during intercourse. If she is orgasmic during nonintercourse sex, she is considered immature or inadequate. Much conflict has been caused by this misunderstanding. Female sexual response is not better or worse than male, but is more complex and variable. The woman can be nonorgasmic, singly orgasmic, or multiorgasmic, which could occur during the pleasuring/foreplay period, during intercourse, or in afterplay. There is not one "right" way to be orgasmic; multiple orgasms are not better than single orgasms; orgasms during intercourse are not better than orgasms with manual, oral, or rubbing stimulation. Physiologically, an orgasm is an orgasm regardless of the means of stimulation. The purported distinction between vaginal and clitoral orgasm is not scientifically valid.

Each couple need to develop their own sexual style. Healthy sexuality is about giving and receiving pleasure rather than a competition to perform for the right kind of orgasm. The goal of sex therapy is to help a woman (and her spouse) develop a sexual style where she is aroused and orgasmic and enjoys intercourse. If she is orgasmic during intercourse, that's fine, and if not, that's fine too. Some women find it easier to be orgasmic during intercourse if they utilize multiple stimulation—for example, self or partner stimulation of the clitoral area, self or partner stimulation of the breasts, use of sexual fantasies, partner stimulation of the labia and/or anal area.

For women who have never been orgasmic, the treatment of choice is self-exploration/masturbation, with the assistance of a vibrator if desired. If she is aware of her arousal and orgasm pattern, the woman may find it easier to share with her spouse. Some women prefer to be orgasmic with intercourse and others prefer and/or find it easier to be orgasmic with manual, oral, or rubbing stimulation. The key is feeling comfortable with sexual expression.

INHIBITED SEXUAL DESIRE

Approximately one in three women complain of inhibited sexual desire, half of those reporting it a lifelong problem. The key elements in sexual desire are positive anticipation and the sense that you deserve satisfying sex. The first task is identifying factors that block desire. Common causes include lack of positive feelings about the body and genitalia; guilt and stigma caused by sexual trauma such as child sexual abuse, incest, rape, guilt over masturbation or non-socially accepted fantasies, being exhibited to or peeped on, being humiliated or rejected; feeling emotionally alienated from the spouse; anger, depression, or anxiety; poor body image; feeling stressed or overwhelmed; seeing sex as primarily for the man; not feeling comfortable with pleasuring and sexual scenarios; fear of loss of control.

In primary inhibited sexual desire, the woman views sexuality as fulfilling the man's needs and desires, not hers. A key concept is her feeling that she "deserves" to have sexual self-esteem and that sexuality can enhance her intimate relationship. She can learn to be an active, involved sexual partner. Her desires and preferences matter. The spouse is viewed as a sexual friend who cares about her feelings and needs, not someone who dominates her or puts her down.

PAINFUL INTERCOURSE AND VAGINISMUS

Almost all woman experience painful intercourse on occasion. This can occur on intromission (entry) or during thrusting. The woman is urged to consult a gynecologist and to be specific about the location, onset, type, and duration of the pain. There are a number of potential medical causes including infection, tears in the vaginal wall, remnants of hymen tissue. Typically, the problem involves psychological factors and sexual technique. The most common causes of pain at intromission are the male misguiding the penis into the vagina or being too rough. The most common cause of pain on thrusting is lack of vaginal lubrication due to low levels of arousal. Why should the male guide intromission? The woman is the expert on her body and can guide his penis into her. The key to arousal is receptivity and responsivity to stimulation. She can make requests and guide his hands and mouth. Use of a lubricant such as K-Y jelly or a nonallergenic lotion with a pleasant smell and texture, facilitates vaginal lubrication.

Vaginismus is rare, but causes a great deal of physical and mental anguish. The good news is that it is successfully treated in ninety percent of women. In vaginismus the vaginal introitus (opening) goes into involuntary spasms so intromission is extremely difficult and painful. In some cases, intercourse is impossible. Vaginismus can be caused by sexual trauma in childhood, rape, fear of the penis, or fear of pregnancy. Treatment combines sexual counseling and vaginal exercises for reconditioning. It is crucial that the woman feel comfortable and in control of her vagina and intercourse.

MALE SEXUAL DYSFUNCTIONS

Sexual dysfunction is more common in women, but more devastating for men. It is a truism that too much of a man's self-esteem is tied to his penis. Sexuality should be fifteen to twenty percent of a person's self-esteem, but for males it's much more. When there is a problem, especially an erectile dysfunction, it can become the dominant factor in a man's life. The most common sexual dysfunctions are:

1. Early ejaculation.
2. Secondary erectile dysfunction.
3. Secondary inhibited sexual desire.
4. Intermittent ejaculatory inhibition.

EARLY EJACULATION

Approximately one in three males has poor ejaculatory control. This varies in severity from ejaculation during intromission to ejaculating within a minute of thrusting. There is not a satisfactory scientific definition of early ejaculation. Perhaps the most useful is that the male does not have voluntary control and early ejaculation causes difficulty in the relationship. Early ejaculation has an excellent prognosis with treatment.

The most common cause of early ejaculation is high sexual arousal combined with anxiety about pleasing the partner. This pattern is a strongly overlearned one. Do-it-yourself techniques aimed at reducing arousal include wearing two or three condoms, using desensitizing cream on the penis, biting the tongue, thinking nonsexual thoughts such as how much money you owe. These techniques serve to distract and reduce arousal, but do not facilitate ejaculatory control.

Learning ejaculatory control is a couple task focusing on increasing awareness and comfort, not reducing arousal. The man has to learn to identify the point of ejaculatory inevitability, after which ejaculation is no longer a voluntary response. The next step involves practicing manual or oral stimulation where he maintains arousal, but does not proceed to the point of ejaculatory inevitability. Techniques include relaxation, enjoying a range of sexual sensations, and increasing sexual comfort. The major technique is "stop-start": as he approaches the point of inevitability, the man tells his partner or nonverbally signals her to stop stimulation until the urge to ejaculate decreases (usually ten to thirty seconds). At first he might need to employ the stop-start ten times in ten minutes, but with practice control increases. The "squeeze" technique originally used has been discarded because it was too clinical and awkward.

Intercourse exercises utilize the woman-on-top position and follow the stop-start format. The woman guides intromission. At first there is no movement (this is called the "quiet vagina" exercise). The male increases awareness and comfort with the sensations of vaginal containment. Movement is initiated by the woman and is slow and nondemanding. If he feels the urge to ejaculate, he tells her to stop. The process gradually includes more movement, the male thrusting, and use of different intercourse positions. It is hardest to maintain ejaculatory control in the man-on-top position with short, rapid stroking. The couple communicates and works together to gradually improve ejaculatory control and mutual enjoyment of intercourse.

SECONDARY ERECTILE DYSFUNCTION

Erectile dysfunction refers to the inability to get or maintain an erection sufficient for intercourse. The major cause is performance anxiety. Sexuality is an active, involving process of giving and receiving pleasure; it is not a spectator sport in which a man passively observes the state of his penis, or a performance with fear of failure. Occasional erectile difficulties are a normal part of male sexuality. This can be caused by a variety of factors including fatigue, alcohol, a side effect of medication, anger, depression, being preoccupied, not feeling sexy but embarrassed to say no, lack of sexual stimulation. Erectile functioning is only problematic when it becomes a frequent pattern. If there is an erection problem in one of four intercourse attempts, the man (and his partner) develop anticipatory anxiety. Erection problems that continue over six months become chronic and severe. No matter what originally caused the difficulty, sex falls into the cycle of negative anticipation, aversive experience, and avoidance.

The key is restoring comfort and confidence with erectile functioning, which is best approached as a couple task. Performance pressure is reduced by placing a temporary prohibition on intercourse. To restore pleasure and sensuality, the couple begin with nondemand touching. Positive anticipation, comfort, pleasure, and arousal is naturally followed by erection—you cannot will or force an erection. Men think of erections as automatic and are used to proceeding to intercourse on the first erection. For most men, experiencing the waxing and waning of erections is new. Being aware of this natural physiological process allows him not to panic when his erection wanes, since he knows that if he stays involved in the pleasuring process, and receptive to stimulation, his erection will again wax (become firm). He can make clear, direct requests for stimulation. If he feels anxious or does not regain an erection, this need not result in an embarrassing failure. He can engage in nonintercourse sex, pleasure his partner, or have a nondemand sensuous experience. In overcoming an erection problem the couple are less critical and demanding and focus on intimacy and pleasure.

INHIBITED SEXUAL DESIRE

This is a common problem for both males and females. For males, almost all sexual desire problems are secondary. Typically, the desire problem is preceded by a sexual dysfunction and/or a rejection. The man no longer anticipates being sexual. He will masturbate (although embarrassed), but suppresses thoughts and fantasies about marital sex. Illness, low testosterone, alcohol or drug abuse, job or family stress, poor health habits, and especially disturbed sleep and lack of exercise, depression, or anger at spouse, can cause desire problems. Once the factors that inhibit desire are identified, they can be challenged and replaced with attitudes, behavior, and emotions that facilitate sexual expression. Men believe sex belongs to the young, is best when illicit, and that the "real man" functions automatically, needing nothing from his partner. Rebuilding desire means not waiting until you magically feel "horny," but building bridges that enhance anticipation and desire. These include intimate talks, increased touching both inside and outside the bedroom, enjoying a range of sexual thoughts and fantasies, viewing sexually oriented movies and reading sexually oriented books or pictorial material, engaging in sensuous activities like showering together or giving/receiving a massage using lotion.

A semi-structured attraction exercise involves the woman sharing what she finds attractive about both his physical and personal attributes. He accepts and acknowledges the compliments, rather than shrugging them off or saying, "Yes, but . . ." She can make one to three requests for change that will make him more attractive to her. They then switch roles where he says what he finds attractive about her and makes requests that would enhance her attractiveness.

Another exercise is for each partner to design and carry out a sexual scenario. For example, he might suggest a pleasuring experience where they take turns touching and she verbalizes sexual thoughts and feelings. During intercourse he can ask her to guide intromission and be on top until he feels highly aroused and then switch positions so he can engage in deep, rapid thrusting. During afterplay, he could ask for a back rub and talk about romantic memories. Each person can design a special scenario.

INTERMITTENT EJACULATORY INHIBITION

Ejaculatory inhibition refers to the male feeling aroused, but not being able to reach orgasm and ejaculate. This occurs very rarely in younger males, but about fifteen percent of men over fifty experience it. The key in overcoming the problem is to identify orgasm triggers such as fantasies, types of stimulation, movements that allow the male to reach orgasm, and use of multiple stimulation during intercourse. Like most sexual dysfunctions, the couple working together as an intimate team increase sexual functioning and satisfaction.

Molly and Brent. This couple had been married four years and came to sex therapy feeling great embarrassment. They had been referred by an infertility specialist because sexual problems interfered with their ability to conceive. They felt doubly stigmatized having both sexual dysfunctions and an infertility problem. Brent had a severe problem with early ejaculation; he ejaculated before his penis was in Molly's vagina. He felt terribly embarrassed and avoided sex, preferring to masturbate instead. Molly had a history of childhood sexual abuse and a primary problem of inhibited sexual desire. She was not distressed by Brent's sexual avoidance because it fitted with her desire dysfunction. However, they wanted children and the sexual problems sabotaged this goal.

The first issue was their sense of demoralization, stigma, and trauma. The therapist established the expectation that sexual avoidance and early ejaculation could be solved and that they would be able to conceive. He raised the question of whether they deserved to have a satisfying sexual relationship and whether they wanted to focus on sexual pleasure or just sexual function. Molly surprised herself (and Brent) by saying she was interested in sexual enjoyment as well as conceiving. She accepted the concept of sex as a couple problem easier than Brent, who held to the belief that he was responsible for all their problems, that if he could only *perform*, everything would be fine. It was this pressured goal-orientation that caused the early ejaculation.

Molly and Brent began with nondemand pleasuring, with Molly approaching touching from a new perspective. Sex was voluntary as opposed to coercive, as it had been in the abuse incidents, and she was actively involved in giving and receiving pleasure. During therapy sessions, she disclosed feelings about the sexual abuse. Brent was able to stop his preoccupation with sexual performance and be an empathetic, caring spouse. With pressure reduced by a temporary prohibition on intercourse, Brent came to enjoy a range of sensual and sexual experiences. In a month, they resumed intercourse. The process of gaining ejaculatory control was gradual, but he did ejaculate intravaginally and after four months they conceived. Just as important, they discovered sexuality could be an intimate part of marriage rather than a source of embarrassment and trauma. They resolved to remain a sexually active couple throughout the pregnancy.

CLOSING THOUGHTS

How important is sexuality in self-esteem and marriage? When sexuality is functional it plays an integral but relatively minor role. Its major function is to energize the marital bond. Sexuality assumes a powerfully negative role when there is a problem. Examples include sexual trauma such as rape or childhood sexual abuse, being obsessed with an extramarital affair, feeling like a failure because of a sexual dysfunction, fear of AIDS, feeling less of a person because of infertility. These issues need to be addressed and resolved, otherwise self-esteem and the marriage are subverted.

Sexuality is a good thing in life, a positive, integral part of you as a person. Sexuality can enhance self-esteem, serve as a shared pleasure, and reinforce marital intimacy.

EIGHT

Family of Origin/Family of Creation

How important is your first family—your family of origin—for self-esteem, marriage, and family of creation? Traditional clinicians believed the unconscious conflicts, unresolved feelings, and hidden trauma from the family of origin was the dominant factor in self-esteem. They thought partner choice and marital satisfaction was strongly influenced, if not controlled, by experiences from the family of origin. Common folklore enforced these themes: "You act just like your father," "If you marry someone from a problem family, you'll inherit all the problems," "What else can you expect, her mother was so possessive." Parents hated to hear that their children were in psychotherapy because they'd be blamed for all the problems. There is a lot of "mother bashing" and "father bashing" in mental health, especially from self-help books and groups. In recent years, the Adult Children of Alcoholics movement has spawned Adult Children of Dysfunctional Families, Adult Children of Violence, Incest Survivors, Adult Children of Divorce, Adult Children of Adulterers.

Throughout this book we emphasize the importance of self-esteem, of taking responsibility and acting in your best interest, living life in the present rather than being controlled by the past. We do recognize that a major factor in self-esteem, for better or worse, is your family of origin. All of us wish we could have grown up like TV families—"The Waltons" or the Huxtables of "The Cosby Show." In these ideal families each parent had high self-esteem and a loving and secure marital bond. The family unit was emotionally cohesive, with each child's worth and self-esteem nurtured. When problems arose they were successfully dealt with in the hour allotted. This is the ideal, but almost no one experiences the ideal family of origin. On the other extreme are writers of the Adult Child theory, who claim that ninety-seven percent of people come from dysfunctional families.

A REALISTIC APPROACH TO FAMILIES OF ORIGIN

The truth for most people is that they come from families with both strengths and weaknesses. Those from families with predominant strengths should be grateful for the positive model, but should also understand that they must devote time and energy to build and reinforce adult self-esteem and create a marriage and family they can be proud of and enjoy. Those who come from difficult families, with a history of physical or sexual abuse or extreme dysfunction, will have to work harder and spend more time and energy developing self-esteem, a viable marriage, and a healthy family. They'll need psychological energy to overcome negative experiences, deficits, and attacks on self-esteem. We are not saying that this is an easy task or that good intentions alone will be enough. It is possible, and indeed necessary, to assume responsibility for developing self-esteem and a family of creation that is healthier than your family of origin. Barry's clinical work involves incest families and adults who were sexually abused as children. His therapeutic theme is to accept, rather than deny, the reality of the abuse, and deal with it so the adult sees herself as a survivor rather than as a victim. The key concept is: "Living well is the best revenge." For this person's marriage and family to succeed, including being sexually healthy, much thought, talk, and work is required in the context of a respectful, trusting, intimate relationship.

We have spent time—as we will ask you to do in the exercises—assessing the positive and negative aspects of each parent's life and marriage as well as the strengths and problems of our childhoods. We have helped each other integrate positive aspects into our lives, marriage, and family of creation and increased awareness of traps to monitor so we don't repeat negative patterns. This has not been easy, but it is worthwhile.

In assessing your family of origin, there are two traps to be aware of. The first is the avoidance trap, in which you look at your background in a superficial manner with a summary such as, "My father was emotionally distant, but my mother was a saint," or "My father was hard-working and responsible and my mother was a worrier." Parents are complex people with individual strengths, weaknesses, and idiosyncracies. Don't make them into simplistic stereotypes. The second trap is to blame all problems on parents. The media emphasis on alcoholism, physical abuse, sexual abuse, workaholics, emotionally unavailable fathers, depressed mothers, and adulterers has become a pop psychology obsession. It would appear that everyone comes from a dysfunctional family, is addicted to something and/or codependent on someone. It is crucially important to understand and accept trauma and problems, but to live in the present and plan for the future, and not to feel victimized by the past. Both the extremes of denial/avoidance and obsession/feeling-controlled rob you of energy needed to build an intimate marital bond and a healthy family of creation.

Families of origin include more than parents. Siblings, grandparents, aunts, uncles, and cousins may play an important role. A significant number of people grew up in blended families when parents divorced, one parent died or left, children were adopted, parents remarried. Some grew up with a variety of stepparents, half-siblings, or several sets of grandparents. For some these were involved and meaningful relationships, while for others they were peripheral. One of Barry's clients had been through a great deal of family therapy with emphasis on the importance of cross-generational patterns. He observed, "In all my therapy no one asked about the people next door, who were like a substitute family and much more important to me than all the extended family put together." As you engage in the self-assessment exercise, be aware of the range of family influences, especially how they affected your self-esteem and your view of marriage and family.

Exercise One: Your Parents and Their Marriage

Each spouse can do this exercise separately and then share it. Take three pieces of paper and draw a line down the middle of each. On the right side of the first page, list the personal attributes of your mother that you liked and respected. Be as specific and objective as possible. On the left side list as specifically as you can her weaknesses and problem areas. There is a tendency to be emotional and subjective (either overly positive or negative). By age twenty-five, most people have developed the maturity to realize that their parents were people first and parents second. Be objective about strengths, weaknesses, and idiosyncracies. The common trap is making global generalizations such as "He was an angry person," or "She was phobic," which rob parents of their individuality and complexity. Generalizations cheat you of insights and understandings. Be specific about times, people, and situations. For example, "My father was angry about work, which he expressed by yelling after drinking with friends. When he wasn't drinking he wouldn't be angry, but was withdrawn." "My mother was comfortable with people, but when she was in a new situation or with people she didn't feel close to she would be anxious to the point of phobia, especially when driving." Be as specific and objective as possible when describing what each was like as a parent. Many people are more comfortable parenting five-year-olds than fifteen-year-olds; list strengths and weaknesses at different stages of parenting.

On the second page, do the same exercise in regard to your father's positive and negative characteristics. Children think of parents as an inseparable unit. In truth, they are individual people. Give serious thought to what your father was like as a person, separate from his role as a father. Then review what you liked and disliked about his parenting.

On the third page, do an objective assessment of the strengths and weaknesses of your parents' marriage. Realize that marriages change over time; be specific about when these characteristics were prominent. Adults from divorced families or marriages that stayed together unhappily until one spouse died have a tendency to focus only on the end product. Even couples who had bitter divorces acknowledge that there were relationship strengths and good times. Be aware of positives and negatives at different stages of the marriage. If your parents' marriage ended in divorce or death, how did they handle the loss and reorganize their lives? What did you learn from observing that process?

If a parent remarried, do this exercise for the second marriage as well. Highlight aspects of the marriage you admired. Then pinpoint components you view as unsuccessful or inappropriate.

After you have completed this exercise, share the lists with your spouse. It also can be valuable to hear the spouse's perceptions of your parents and their marriage, especially if he is objective and specific. You do not have to agree—after all, they're your parents—but it can broaden your perspective. Respect the spouse's confidence; don't throw disclosures back at her during a fight. One advantage of an intimate marriage is that you can share concerns and vulnerabilities without fear of being taken advantage of.

View your parents in a realistic, objective light. Perhaps this will help you deal more effectively with your aging parents. Knowledge is power. Increasing awareness of the strengths and weaknesses of your family of origin allows you to increase self-esteem and develop a loving and satisfying family of creation.

Donna and Art. Donna and Art, in their mid-forties, felt sandwiched between two generations—aging parents and growing children. They married in their twenties and had children in their early thirties. Kim was now fourteen and Jack eleven. Donna's father had died four years before, her mother was seventy-three and in good health. Art's parents were divorced. His mother, who was seventy-four, had not remarried; his seventy-five-year-old father had remarried, but his second wife had left the year before.

Donna and Art had very different approaches to their families of origin, influenced in part by gender socialization. Donna kept close contact with her mother, siblings, and extended family. She talked regularly with her mother, and valued the insights derived from these discussions. She'd had a close, yet volatile, relationship with her father, who had wanted Donna to become a doctor rather than a physical therapist. He had promoted high standards, and Donna felt he had not approved of her life choices. Her mother kept assuring Donna that her father had admired her career and family. Donna deeply regretted not having talked more with him. She wished she'd told him how important he'd been, what she valued and respected, as well as her resentments. Most of all, she wished she'd asked what he really thought of her. Donna wanted Kim and Jack to talk directly to Art; she would not play the role of middleman or interpreter.

Art avoided his parents, especially his father. He was closest to an older sister and her family, but maintained distance from a younger brother who had a multitude of marital and financial problems. Donna was closer to her mother-in-law than Art was. Art wanted to be a better father to Kim and Jack than his father had been to him. However, he was often short-tempered with Jack, and it was clear that he preferred Kim.

Donna was frustrated because she wanted to discuss family and marital issues seriously, but Art would laugh the subject off. He joked that if he began to act like his father she should throw him out. Art accused Donna of wanting to overanalyze the past. Donna counterattacked that Art wanted to avoid and deny problems.

Following cultural tradition, Donna and Art were more involved with her family. It was Donna's responsibility to keep contact with both sides of the extended family. The grandmothers were more involved with the grandchildren than the grandfathers. Donna was pleased that her mother and mother-in-law were interested and involved in Kim's life. They were less involved with Jack, which was a loss for the son as well as his grandparents. Donna felt bad that her children had few significant memories of their maternal grandfather, who had been quite ill and weak the year before his death. She herself had fond memories of her father playing with Kim and Jack when they were babies, but the children didn't recall much. Neither Art nor Donna promoted contact with the other grandfather who remained emotionally distant and self-absorbed with health problems.

Donna fell into the common female trap of feeling overly responsible for family members. It is hard to maintain a balance between being involved and concerned, but not burdened and overresponsible. Donna's attempts to make everything okay interfered with her enjoyment of her family. She was so concerned with not playing favorites that she didn't spend enough time with the adults and children she most enjoyed. Her sister confronted Donna about doing too much for too many people; she needed to enjoy the family and get something from it rather than always giving. Between marriage, children, work, house, and extended family, she spread herself too thin. Art reinforced what the sister said. Donna agreed, but resented Art for not assuming more family and household responsibilities.

Art was in the common male trap of keeping family at a distance. When he did interact it was about practical and financial matters, rather than sharing feelings, telling stories, or exchanging perceptions. Art did have a favorite nephew (his sister's son), whom he took on family excursions and who was like an older brother to Jack.

The pattern of avoidance was confronted when Art's father

became terminally ill. Donna and his sister encouraged Art to make peace with his father before he died. Visiting the father in the hospital was a most difficult emotional experience. Art and his father colluded in talking about financial and legal matters rather than discussing the dying process. Practical matters can be used to avoid dealing with emotions and saying goodbye. Finally, Art had the courage to ask his father the two questions he'd always wanted to ask—whether his father had enjoyed parenting Art and whether his father regretted marrying Art's mother. His father's responses were not as self-disclosing as Art wished, but gave him important insights. What had the most emotional impact was his father saying he wished he'd spent more time with his children as they were growing up and urging Art to be more involved with Jack and Kim. Art was not able to cry with his father, but as he told this to Donna he cried. Art realized a parent is first a person, with his own strengths and weaknesses. Art was determined to be a better father, especially to Jack, than his father had been to him.

The first time Kim and Jack saw their father cry was at the funeral. They had not felt close to their grandfather, but did appreciate the stories they'd heard about their dad's growing up. It is healthy for children to have a sense of the reality and complexity of the extended family. The grandmother attended the funeral and was able to share stories without rancor or bitterness. Wakes and funerals bring out the best and worst in families. Art's younger brother continued to be alienated, and on a couple of occasions was quite obnoxious. That too is the reality of extended families.

Death can motivate people to live their lives in a more fulfilling manner. Art appreciated the emotional support he received from Donna. They talked not only of his family of origin, but hopes and desires for their family of creation. As they disclosed feelings, perceptions, hopes, and fears, emotional intimacy increased. Donna realized these were not just her concerns, but were shared with Art. He needed to be aware of vulnerabilities from his family of origin so as not to fall into these traps in his life and family. Art felt awkward and self-conscious about disclosing feelings and perceptions, especially about marital and family issues. To facilitate this they set a "communication date," to sit on their porch Wednesday nights to disclose and share feelings and fears. They purposely stayed away from discussing money, jobs, and houses.

Art's being aware of and attending to family matters relieved pressure on Donna. She relaxed and enjoyed family activities. They decided to go away as a couple without children at least one weekend a year. Art's sister thought that was a great idea and agreed to watch their children.

Art and Donna had followed a traditional pattern of the mother being the primary parent. Donna loved parenting and did not want to lessen her involvement, but welcomed Art's increased activity. He enjoyed taking the children places, especially to soccer and basketball games. He also brought them to his jobs and explained what he did as a landscape architect. He wanted to develop a shared hobby with Jack, and asked him for ideas. Jack was enthusiastic about building model planes. Having a project allowed Art to spend more time with his son and be less critical. Art's involvement allowed Donna to do things one-on-one with Kim rather than always splitting her time. Kim especially enjoyed the mother-daughter tennis group. One of Donna's goals was to establish a better life balance, including time for herself. Balancing self-esteem, marriage, family of creation, and extended family is not easy, but it is worthwhile.

DYSFUNCTIONAL FAMILIES OF ORIGIN

The movement that began with Adult Children of Alcoholics has spread to groups such as Adult Children of Divorce, Adult Children of Violence, and the generic Adult Children of Dysfunctional Families. The pendulum has swung from the myth of the perfect "Ozzie and Harriet" family to the "ninety-seven percent of families are dysfunctional" myth. In truth, all families have strengths and all have problems. Some families, especially those caught in the traps of addiction, violence, sexual abuse, mental illness, and/or poverty, are dysfunctional. Does growing up in a severely dysfunctional family control self-esteem and result in the inability to create a functional and healthy family of your own? Theoretically, clinically, and personally, we strongly believe the answer is no. You do need to be aware of psychological traps and to devote more time and energy to develop self-esteem, a strong marital bond, and a rewarding family of creation.

Exercise Two: Integrating Positive Aspects of Your Family of Origin and Monitoring Traps

Be sure you have completed the first exercise and have gotten feedback from your spouse. The purpose of the first exercise was to view your parents and their marriage objectively. The purpose of this exercise is to take your increased awareness and apply it to self-esteem, marriage, and family of creation. As you review the positive attributes of each parent, especially your same sex parent, pick at least two characteristics you would like to integrate into your life. Be specific about how they would function in your life. Consider the positive attributes of the marital model. Choose at least two characteristics to emulate in your marriage. How can you integrate them and how can your spouse facilitate the process? Consider two positive attributes of parenting. How can you parent your children so they receive the positive benefits of this way of growing up and these parenting techniques?

In outlining traps to monitor, it is even more important to be specific. Remember, this is not a parent-blaming exercise, but an attempt to improve self-esteem and family of creation. Be aware of two negative characteristics to monitor carefully so that they are not repeated in your marriage and family of creation. In monitoring traps, awareness is important, but even more crucial is a commitment to a positive pattern of thinking, acting, and expressing emotion that counteracts these characteristics. Don't strive to develop a perfect marriage and family of creation, but to do better than your parents, with the hope that your children will benefit and do better than you.

A RESPECTFUL VIEW OF FAMILY OF ORIGIN

Many people find this approach to the family of origin profoundly upsetting. They question what has happened to family pride, ethnic roots, or family tradition. They fear this is so analytical that it cuts out the core of families. We are sensitive to this concern. Pendulums swing from one extreme to the other. It is no more helpful or true, to denigrate and negate the family of origin than to put it on a pedestal.

If these guidelines are to be helpful, stay focused on the positive motivation of increasing awareness and understanding family patterns. Positive motivation promotes self-esteem and helps in developing a satisfying family of creation. People learn more if they approach their family of origin in a respectful manner, with a sense of empathy rather than blame. We feel strongly about this, although it contrasts with traditional psychodynamic approaches and with the victimization-oriented Adult Child theory. It is crucial to deal with the reality of your family of origin without denying or minimizing problems. However, it is not helpful to feel stuck in the victim role. Don't define your life and self-esteem by childhood abuse. The person needs to view himself as a survivor, not a victim. Base self-esteem and family of creation on the premise that you deserve to have a more respectful, successful life than your family of origin.

No matter what the media hype, the truth is that most families were not abusive. What is true is that *every* family had its problems, weaknesses, and areas of dysfunction. Part of self-respect is accepting your family of origin with greater objectivity, increasing awareness of strengths and weaknesses. Strive for a functional and satisfying family of creation, the most important ingredients being an intimate marriage and parenting as a cooperative team.

Terry and Holly. This was Terry's first marriage and Holly's second. When married sixteen years before, Terry and Holly were very optimistic about their ability to have a successful marriage and family. Holly had sole custody of Todd, her three-year-old son. She and Terry planned, and had, two additional children, and then Holly had a tubal ligation. Their children are now nineteen, fifteen, and fourteen.

Terry and Holly perceive both their family of origin and family of creation much differently than sixteen years ago. Although they continue to feel good about their marriage and family, they realize how naïve they had been. Terry had felt confident that there would be no difference between his adopted son and biological daughters. As Todd entered adolescence, though, he made it clear he felt a difference. His biological father had remarried and wanted to play a role in Todd's life, and Todd wanted to know him. This was threatening for Terry and Holly. Terry reacted like a hurt and angry adolescent, feeling that Todd's interest was a rejection of him. The daughters tried to help Terry put this in perspective, but he felt insecure in his role as Todd's father. Holly had angry feelings about the husband who had abandoned her with a child and no money. She knew it was not psychologically healthy for Todd to hear his father disparaged, but she wanted to tell at least a couple of horror stories. Adding to Holly's distress was that her daughters liked Todd's father. This unexpected disruption in their family convinced Terry and Holly to consult a family therapist who saw the family together, including all three children.

Adolescence can be a tumultuous period for the adolescent and parents alike. Ideally, families would have a sense of emotional cohesion with flexibility of roles and respect for individuality. Adolescence is a time of defining oneself and the peer group supplanting the family. It is a time for the adolescent to challenge family boundaries and rules. In the pressure to define self, there is a decrease in empathy for others, especially parents. Terry and Holly were idealistic parents of young children, a period they thoroughly enjoyed.

However, they felt ill-prepared for adolescence, a time that strains parental idealism. Todd's search to understand and develop a relationship with his biological father was the most difficult part of a stressful process.

The family therapist was helpful in putting this process in perspective. She helped Terry and Holly to avoid going from an idealistic extreme to an extreme of cynicism and negation. Todd needed their understanding and permission to explore what kind of relationship he could develop with his biological father. Terry had to realize that Todd's interest was not a negation of Terry's role as an adoptive father. Holly had to realize that her ex-husband had matured. Rather than fighting the old battles again, she had to view his relationship with Todd in a new light. The family therapist made Terry and Holly aware that each daughter had individual needs and it would be helpful not to view the "girls" together as if they were one entity, and helpful to the entire family if there was a less intense focus on Todd. Families are like individuals: they go through phases of problems, change, and growth. Families can't rest on their laurels. Terry and Holly had put a lot of time and energy into creating a "perfect" family. In truth, no family is perfect. They had to regroup and accept that they'd made mistakes, but without negating the good things they'd experienced and shared. The family therapist gave Terry the task of talking with his own father to help him resolve issues from his family of origin. This helped him see that Todd's struggles were part of a normal process of becoming an individual. The therapist gave Holly the task of looking back on her family of origin and first marriage and viewing them with greater complexity and clarity than the black-white picture she had projected. When an individual takes simplistic positions, she ignores the complex reality of people's lifes; this was the trap Holly had fallen into. Slogans like "Today is the first day of the rest of your life," "Be all that you can be," "Create yourself," are not necessarily bad, but taken to the extreme as Holly had done, were problematic. She set herself up to overpromise and overexpect, with the result that she felt disillusioned and depressed.

There was much in Holly's life, marriage, and family that she could feel proud of. You have to be aware of continuities in life. You cannot create or totally remake yourself. Present ideas, behavior, feelings, and experiences need to be integrated with your past, without negating the past. Self-esteem is about integration, not denial or pretending.

The therapist reminded Terry and Holly that in just six short years they would be a couple again when their youngest daughter left for college (education was highly valued in their family). The husband-wife bond is the most important in a family, and during this stressful period, it had been neglected. Lack of attention to the marriage had made them more vulnerable and insecure about problems with Todd. Taking a weekend away, without children, was the best thing they did that year. They agreed to spend the first two days talking about themselves, their lives and feelings, and not discuss adolescent and parenting issues until Sunday afternoon. They used the time to exercise, sleep late, make love, explore mountain trails, and have a gourmet meal in a romantic setting. They returned energized to deal with the complex issues of their family of creation, but kept them in perspective. This was beneficial for Todd and the rest of the family.

CLOSING THOUGHTS

We could write an entire book—and hope to—about the complex interrelationships of self-esteem, family of origin, and family of creation. We believe in guidelines, but don't want to fall into Holly's trap of leading life based on slogans and one-liners. With that caveat, here are our guidelines: Life is meant to be lived in the present with planning for the future, not feeling victimized and controlled by the past. You are responsible for your life, marriage, and family of creation. Viewing your family of origin with objectivity and empathy facilitates gathering information and resources to better understand and direct your life. For individuals and couples from severely dysfunctional families these guidelines are even more relevant. Coming from a dysfunctional family means that you need to be aware of traps, and devote more time and psychological resources to establish self-esteem, an intimate and secure marriage, and a successful family of creation.

NINE

Is Staying Together Healthy for Self-Esteem?

Couples usually separate in a highly emotional, explosive manner. The coming apart results from a fight, discovery of an extramarital affair, or a confrontation over a long-simmering problem. It's as if the couple need something powerful to propel them out of the marriage; it can't be a rational, talked-out decision.

Empirical studies show that the divorce process extends over a two-year period. Separation and divorce has been labeled a "crazy time" because conflicting feelings and desires put you on an extended emotional roller-coaster. You wonder if you'll be able to stand it. People do survive divorce, but it is a bruising experience. Divorce has been likened to war; it leaves scars and the disruption lasts long after the last shot is fired. How do you decide if it's worth going to the divorce war?

The crucial question is the viability of this marriage. The key is whether the marriage promotes or subverts each spouse's self-esteem. When Barry is practicing therapy with a married couple he conceptualizes there being three clients—each individual and the marital bond. Ideally, therapy would enhance each person's self-esteem and revitalize the marital bond. However, there are marriages where this is impossible. The marriage exists at the expense of one or both spouse's self-esteem. An example is the caretaker marriage. The man might be highly dysfunctional: severely depressed, alcoholic, a sociopathic personality, suffering from schizophrenia. The woman takes care of him by pretending everything is fine and covering up his failings. She claims to need his strength and that she can't live without him. In reality, he needs her and both are afraid he'd fall apart without the marriage. Another example is a marriage controlled by one spouse's problem. The woman's agoraphobia defines her life and the couple's activities. Her role in the family is that of patient. The husband puts her down and knowingly or unknowingly interferes with her progress in confronting fears and becoming independent. He is comfortable with her being the problem person and he the benevolent, long-suffering spouse. These are unhealthy marriages. Sometimes the marriage can survive if spouses dramatically change their roles and self-definition. However, often the roles are set in concrete and the only way to break the impasse is to end the marriage.

THE DECISION PROCESS

College students say that if a marriage is not working, people should just get a divorce. It sounds so easy. In truth, it is an agonizing decision, and it's even harder to go through the difficult and draining divorce process. Yet, sometimes it is absolutely necessary in order to preserve or regain self-esteem. Seldom is the decision to separate mutual; seldom is the decision to stay together an individual one. Each spouse must choose based on what is in his/her best interest. In the past, couples were urged to remain married no matter what. There were powerful community, religious, and extended family pressures against divorce. This began changing in the 1960s. Divorce was hailed as the solution to life problems, a symbol of personal growth and the courage to be on your own. As happens when the pendulum swings from one extreme to another, the overpromise of success and happiness does not occur and there is a counter-movement. The United States has one of the highest divorce rates, as well as one of the highest remarriage rates, in the world. Divorcing and being on your own, especially as a single parent, is not as easy as promised nor is it the solution to self-esteem problems. We do not advocate returning to the tradition of staying married for the sake of the children or because it is socially correct. Each person has to assess the effect of the marriage on his/her self-esteem and must determine if the marital bond of respect, trust, and intimacy can be revitalized.

When Barry conducts couples therapy his suggestion to clients is that they assume the marital bond can be revitalized, and that they make a commitment to a six-month good-faith effort to improve the marriage and increase each spouse's self-esteem. During the assessment phase (a couple session and an individual session with each spouse), Barry realizes that for some couples this is not possible. The amount of disrespect and distrust is so great that trying to work on the marriage would be a travesty. For others, a couples contract would be a sham—one spouse is committed to an extramarital affair, there is a major secret such as homosexual orientation or an illegal business deal, or this is a marriage of convenience with no desire to build intimacy. In some situations an individual issue—an acute psychotic episode, a religious crisis, a diagnosis of cancer—is so dominant that there is no psychological energy to deal with marital issues, which can be addressed later. Some individuals need all their psychological and practical energy to manage their lives, leaving little for the marriage. The spouse has to ask himself whether it is in his best interest to stay married under these circumstances.

A common pattern is the marginal marriage. One spouse, usually the husband, values the social acceptability of being married and having a home, with or without children. He expects little from the marriage and gives little of himself to it. His focus is on career, sports or hobby, politics or religion, or being a self-contained person. He has a low need for intimacy or gets sexual needs met through an affair. His wife and marriage occupy a small, contained place. The question is whether this marriage meets the woman's needs or is a drain on self-esteem. Both the traditional ideology and a plethora of self-help books aimed at women are full of advice on how she can get the man involved in the marriage. The assumption is it's the woman's role and responsibility to keep her husband happy so he'll stay married. It is her failing if he maintains the marriage in a marginal manner. In our opinion, it is neither the woman's role nor her responsibility. It is her decision whether this marriage meets self-esteem and intimacy needs.

Closely akin to the marginal marriage is the marriage of convenience. What binds the couple is children, house, standing in the community, religious beliefs, money, or protecting one spouse (for example, a gay man who maintains a marriage and has a secret sexual life). The couple's emotional bond is weak. The advantage of a marriage of convenience is stability and predictability; little is asked from either spouse. There is a great deal of personal autonomy, with self-esteem needs being met through other sources. However, the marriage has a built-in risk. The other spouse could fall in love with someone else because of the lack of intimate connection. If there is a crisis, such as a child becoming ill or the spouse losing a job, the other may realize how lacking the marriage is. There is little emotional reservoir to deal with the crisis. Any challenge to the predictable, stable marriage of convenience can break it apart.

A most painful marriage is one in which there had been an intimate marital bond that has shriveled into chronic dissatisfaction. The couple, once close and sharing, now argue, blame, and are glad when the spouse travels on business. Attempts to reconnect and rekindle feelings succeed for a few days, only to be dashed by the next misunderstanding. This is followed by a cycle of blaming, anger, and depression. They recall "the good old days" and dream of "what could have been." Lost hopes and opportunities are particularly grating. If this marriage is to be revitalized, the couple need to focus on the present and future rather than argue about past mistakes or mourn the "what ifs." Is the marital bond broken or still alive, even if badly strained? Can this marriage facilitate self-esteem or does the disappointment and anger keep the couple in a perpetual struggle, draining self-esteem?

How does a couple decide that there are no perfect marriages and that they need to work to make this one viable, even if not totally satisfying? When do they accept that this marriage is not viable and it's time to begin the separation and divorce process? If you decide the latter, don't expect your spouse's consent. Divorce requires one person to take the initiative and leave. The other feels judged and abandoned and experiences lowered self-esteem and he/she tries to fight the end of the marriage. His/her increasingly desperate attempts to win the spouse back further lowers self-esteem. It's easier being the leaver than being left, clinging to the hope of a reconciliation.

Bill and Arlene. Arlene believed the cultural myth that it is men who leave women. During their four-year marriage, she worried that Bill would have an affair and leave her for another woman. Arlene still cannot believe she left Bill. She did not leave for another man, but did use an affair as a stepping stone to separation.

Arlene married at twenty-eight, which is normal for women of her generation. Her mother and older relatives, who had married in their late teens or early twenties, worried that all the good men would be taken. Arlene wanted children, and was as interested in being a parent as a spouse.

During college she insisted that she wouldn't marry young. She achieved B and B+ grades, and enjoyed the easy socializing and parties. She loved meeting people and was fascinated by their differences and motivations. She liked having a boyfriend, but had no desire to live with a man or be engaged. She valued freedom—the access to new people, ideas, and opportunities. After graduation, Arlene moved to Columbus, Ohio. She was employed as an analyst with a large brokerage firm, working hard and playing hard in the singles scene.

After two years, the shine began to wear off her lifestyle and Arlene at age twenty-four felt the need to settle down. In Hollywood stories, the man and moment are supposed to come together, but real life is more complicated. One of the worst mistakes people make is to decide "This is the time to get married." When it doesn't happen, there is a sense of frustration, cynicism, and then panic. It was the latter emotion that caused Arlene to seek out Bill, three weeks after her twenty-sixth birthday.

Bill was thirty-eight and had been single for three years after leaving a four-year marriage. Friends described him as bright, ambitious, and a real character. Arlene remembers mixed feelings the night they met—he was handsome and the life of the party, but too loud, bordering on the hysteric. But she was panicky about getting older and not being married, and this overrode her ambivalence. Being with Bill was an adventure filled with excitement and angst. He was seductive and fun, but elusive, and he put his needs first. He worked hard and played harder. His professional training was in accounting, but he was anything but the stereotypical staid accountant. Bill was an entrepreneur who put together business deals. He was an avid golfer, boater, and partier who added spice to Arlene's life. Late at night after drinking, he told Arlene stories about himself and his first marriage that made her feel closer to him. Genuine self-disclosure is a crucial ingredient in mate selection, but it requires sobriety: be very suspect of self-disclosures occurring when the person is drunk or high.

Arlene pursued Bill. When she tired of his inconsistency and unreliability and began to sour on the relationship, he would do something special that reenergized her pursuit. Arlene became so involved in trying to entice Bill into marriage that she lost track of whether they were a couple for whom respect, trust, and intimacy would grow. Arlene believed that when married Bill would make "magical" changes. Their roller-coaster courtship resulted in an extravagant wedding. It may not have been a "magical marriage," but it was a "magical wedding."

Arlene and Bill made the mistake that is mirrored in many couples: they did not talk about hard issues before marrying. Especially notable was the lack of any discussion of finances and sexual involvement with others. Bill bragged about his deals, but when it came to couple financial decisions he was closed-mouthed and miserly. They lived on Arlene's salary because Bill claimed he needed all the available capital for business deals. He rented his house and they lived in her condo.

Arlene worried about Bill's flirting and rumors of affairs. He labeled this her problem of irrational jealousy, but Arlene felt he enjoyed playing her for a fool. She did not trust him or respect herself for not effectively confronting the issue.

Arlene was using the birth control pill, but wanted a child. Bill said there was too much going on to even talk about it. She made a unilateral decision to discontinue the pill and not tell Bill. She was over three months pregnant and had shared this with her parents and good friends before telling him. As expected he was unhappy, but in a move she did not expect, urged her to get an abortion. Arlene hated confrontations and usually acquiesced in order to avoid ugly scenes. This time she strongly stated her desire to have the child and resisted his pressure. After four weeks, he let it drop. Throughout the pregnancy, Bill kept emotional distance (Arlene later learned he'd had an affair before, during, and after the pregnancy). He would not attend prepared childbirth classes nor was he present at the birth of his daughter. However, he did host a party for social and business acquaintances to celebrate her first month birthday. Arlene gave up trying to interest Bill in sharing parenting tasks. The only thing he did willingly was push the stroller on neighborhood walks.

With a baby, the one-bedroom condo was crowded. Bill was adamant that financially it was not the time to buy a house. With great resentment, Arlene asked her parents for a loan to buy a three-bedroom townhouse.

Arlene was happy with much of her life—her career was progressing, she loved parenting and had an excellent child care person, the townhouse was a fine place to live, and she enjoyed friends and their children. The areas of dissatisfaction were her marriage, finances, and fears about Bill's affairs. Arlene believed the myth that sex was the best barometer of a relationship. Sex with Bill was satisfying, so she felt that theirs was still a loving marriage. The truth is that love and sex are different dimensions—you can be sexually desirous and responsive with a spouse and not feel intimate or trusting.

When Arlene talked to friends about her marital dissatisfaction, they minimized it or told stories about their spouses. One friend, Margie, did listen and validated Arlene's feelings. Margie's husband worked for a bank, questioned Bill's business dealings, and had heard rumors of his affairs. Arlene did not want to be a divorced woman with a child. She urged Bill to enter marriage therapy, but he said it was a waste of money, that psychologists were "kooks."

Two things disrupted the uneasy equilibrium. Arlene met a man through work and the friendship turned into a sexual affair. He knew Bill and had dated a woman Bill had had an affair with. Arlene learned that she could be sexually responsive with another man, although she didn't kid herself about being in love. A month later, one of Bill's business partners was arrested for filing false tax returns. Bill was involved in this and other questionable business transactions. He insisted Arlene take a home equity line of credit on the townhouse.

Marginal marriages can continue for many years until confronted by a crisis—whether this involves a child, an affair, or finances. To survive the crisis, each person must retain a sense of respect and trust in the spouse. Arlene had little respect for Bill and no trust. He had not put any money into the townhouse, yet wanted money from a home equity loan. It was too much to tolerate. With the support of her parents and Margie, Arlene said no. Bill reacted by storming out. Arlene changed the locks and consulted a lawyer. The affair enabled her to make the break and stay with her resolve. The following three months were a crazy roller-coaster, with talk of reuniting and threats of violence. The longer she was away from Bill, the clearer it became to Arlene that being married to him had drained her self-esteem. He had intimidated and controlled her, but did not have her best interests in mind.

The divorce process dragged on for three years, with much legal and financial wrangling. Divorce is difficult for self-esteem, as Arlene can readily testify, but once she became convinced that the marriage was not viable, she knew the road to restore self-esteem was through divorce. She had to reestablish herself as a single-again person responsible for her life, child, house, and financial welfare.

DIVORCE AND SELF-ESTEEM

We are not pro-divorce, but believe divorce is the most viable alternative for an alienated or destructive marriage. A marriage that undermines self-esteem is not worthwhile. Couples in difficult marriages have chronic problems that cannot be fully resolved. Those who stay married accept these difficulties and focus on other satisfactions and sources of self-esteem. The positive attributes of the spouse and strengths of the marriage outweigh dissatisfactions and problems. As we say repeatedly, there are no perfect people and no perfect marriages. It's a myth (fed by movies, talk shows, and self-help books) that if the couple communicate and are more loving they will reach total happiness and perfection.

For a marriage to be viable it has to support each spouse's self-esteem and bolster the intimate bond. Difficulties and problem areas are not secret nor do the couple pretend everything is perfect. They acknowledge difficulties, but maintain a sense of personal integrity, caring, and an intimate bond.

Loss of respect is the first step in the divorce process. If this is not reversed, it means the end of marital satisfaction.

The same is true of trust: unless the trust bond is revitalized the marriage will wither. Intimacy problems are usually a result, rather than a cause, of marital dissatisfaction.

Couples need to address problems, although it is rare to achieve total change. Total cures only happen in movies and novels. One spouse makes significant changes in his behavior, the other makes complementary changes. The couple increase understanding and acceptance and affirm the marriage. For example, therapy is initiated to deal with an eating disorder on the wife's part and the husband's early ejaculation. It is the exception rather than the rule that they become the healthiest, sexiest couple in the community. More commonly, the woman gains control of her eating and the man gains confidence with ejaculatory control. They understand and value each other, but the man wishes that eating and food wasn't such a big issue and the woman wishes that she could be more spontaneous and that sex was easier.

Exercise: A Cost-Benefit Analysis of this Marriage

This is meant to be an individual exercise, and the couple might well decide not to share their analyses. It is a complex and lengthy exercise, but the decision of whether to remain married is vitally important. You'll need at least an hour and three pieces of paper. On the first page, your focus is on the period before you married, on the second page, the present time, and on the third page your projection two years in the future if you stay married. Divide each paper into two columns, one positive, the other negative. On the paper about the past, in the positive column state strengths and satisfactions with single life and what you hoped for in the marriage. In the negative column, state personal problems and concerns you had before marriage and your worst fears about this marriage. Follow the same format for the present, emphasizing specific personal and couple strengths and hopes, as well as problems and fears. As you project this two years into the future on the third page, be realistic about strengths and problem areas, as well as hopes for change and fears of further degeneration.

Sit back and evaluate what you've written. What are the patterns and trends? Did your premarital fears come true? How many of your hopes were fulfilled and how many of your concerns were warranted? Were the positives as rewarding as you thought? Has self-esteem gone up or down? Where is self-esteem heading in the next two years if you stay married? What do you value about the spouse and marriage—has this changed during the course of the marriage? What are the major disappointments and frustrations? Can they be accepted and integrated, or have they done irreparable harm? Would it be constructive to share parts or the entire list with your spouse?

James and Karen. The best time to deal with a problem is when it arises. Problems that fester for years drain self-esteem and reduce marital satisfaction. Resentment, anger and alienation become powerful and controlling.

James was a fifty-four-year-old portfolio manager in the trust department of a large bank and Karen was a fifty-six-year-old economist working for a consulting firm. They were viewed by colleagues, friends, and adult children with admiration bordering on awe. They were healthy, wealthy, and wise, with a beautiful house and, outwardly, a great marriage. However, behind closed doors there was emotional and sexual alienation that had lasted twenty-two years.

The specific incident was an acquaintance rape. The feelings caused by this trauma had never been dealt with. James and Karen had not had intercourse for twelve years; James had a severe erection problem for over twenty years, which began about a year and a half after the rape. Eight years before, the last time they attempted to be sexual, James had lost his erection while trying to insert and had thrown a pillow in Karen's face. They continued to be affectionate in public, but touching while alone was limited and tentative.

What brought them to psychotherapy were physical complaints attributed to job-related stress. The internist suggested therapy because symptoms of fatigue, headaches, weight gain, and back pain indicate a psychosomatic origin (the physical problems are real but are caused primarily by psychological distress). The physician rightly hypothesized that marital problems played a major role.

James and Karen were reluctant and unconvinced clients. They were intellectually bright people, but psychologically denied the chronic conflict and demoralization. A year earlier they'd had a six-month trial of antidepressant medication which James discontinued because of side effects and because he didn't like being dependent on medication. Karen stopped because, even with an elevated mood, her physical problems were not significantly relieved nor did medication address the dissatisfaction.

Karen came from a difficult family of origin with unhappy parents who separated a month after she left for college. She resented that they'd stayed together for her sake. Her college experience was disrupted by the divorce, she felt caught in the middle, and married at twenty hoping to establish a sense of worth and stability. Marriage as a rescue effort has at least two strikes against it. Karen discovered that her husband had lied about completing his degree, and this served as the third strike. She left the marriage after eight months, returned to school part time, and eventually completed her degree. Later, when her children were in school, Karen completed a master's degree in economics. Her academic and professional achievements, as well as parenting, house, and close friends provided the core of Karen's self-esteem.

James's approach to life and education was mainstream, the classic story of a poor boy who made good. He came from a working class, small-town, Midwestern background and entered the navy directly from high school. He used veterans' benefits to obtain a college degree in finance, worked his way up the hierarchy in one bank and switched jobs to a larger, more prestigious bank. James gave the impression of being a rational, well-controlled, self-assured person. He was twenty-six and felt ready to marry when he met

Karen. He felt sure that she would benefit from the strength and stability he provided, and saw her as an attractive, gregarious, and socially involved person who would advance his professional and social life. For James, marriage was a dream come true.

He wanted three children, hoped for sons, and got his wish. He felt successful—in control of his life, career, marriage, and family. James had a pattern of minimizing personal and marital problems. The best example was his underplaying of sexual difficulties. He maintained that there was nothing wrong even though sex was infrequent, about once every two or three weeks, and not particularly satisfying or intimate. Intercourse was functional, but the quality of lovemaking was mediocre at best.

In retrospect, Karen and James had a marginally intimate marriage. It met James's needs more than Karen's—his self-esteem was high, while hers was decreasing. The marital bond was becoming frayed. They were not in a position to cope with the stress caused by the acquaintance rape.

It is common to blame the victim in rape cases, which is intensified if the woman knows the man. The perpetrator was a neighbor well-known for having a drinking problem, who was ostracized in the neighborhood. His youngest son was a friend of Karen's oldest son and Karen tried to be cordial. They attended a picnic celebrating the end of the children's soccer season. As usual, the neighbor drank too much. James left the picnic early to go to his office and complete a report. After he left, an argument broke out between the neighbor and his wife, which disrupted the picnic and caused its premature end. The neighbor's son asked to go back to Karen's house and she agreed because the boys played well together. About an hour later the neighbor appeared. Karen felt uncomfortable, and unwisely offered him a beer. When Karen was unsure, her coping style was to become passive but maintain a friendly demeanor. Three beers later, the neighbor began touching her and ultimately forced her to have intercourse in the den. Karen tried to resist, but felt overwhelmed and ineffective. Her first reaction was to deny the experience and pretend it hadn't happened. The boys had seen part of the incident, although not the actual intercourse.

The story got back to the neighbor's wife and eventually to James. James was angry and blaming, more of Karen than the neighbor. James valued being rational, in control, and appropriate. He resented the gossip and innuendo, and wanted the incident to go away. James and Karen never discussed it, nor did James ask Karen about her feelings. There was one late night argument during which he screamed and she cried. He told her she was stupid, and that he didn't want to hear about it again.

An issue that is not dealt with in a respectful, caring manner becomes a chronic problem that festers and poisons the marriage. Karen and James continued to be sexual on an intermittent basis. However, there was increasing tension and emotional distance. Karen felt victimized, with strong feelings of guilt and humiliation. She felt blamed and shamed by James, and became sexually passive. James could pretend nothing was wrong, but his penis couldn't. He developed an erection problem. Performance anxiety quickly built and in a short time he was trapped in the cycle of negative anticipation, performance failure, and sexual avoidance. They became a nonsexual couple, their energy going into parenting, careers, and the house.

The "empty nest" stage is a good time for most couples. It is a period of personal freedom and opportunity to enhance self-esteem. For Karen, it was a lonely time because she missed the rewards of parenting and felt undervalued in the marriage. She felt she had a choice of remaining married and becoming increasingly depressed, or divorcing. She worried about the effects of divorce on her adult children. She did not want to repeat the pattern of her family of origin. Her feelings toward James were highly ambivalent—there were things she liked and respected, but she was filled with resentment and alienation. She was not as concerned about the lack of sex, although she experienced sexual desire and masturbated one to three times a month. She found James a cold person and bitterly resented that the only times he touched her were in public.

James tried to pretend everything was fine in his life and marriage. He took pride in work, was active in community organizations, and was overly concerned with his sons' achievements and pressured them to strive for greater success. James had gone to prostitutes three times; he'd had erections during fellatio, but not intercourse. James was aware of the AIDS epidemic and wore condoms, but did not like the risks inherent in going to a prostitute. He masturbated one or two times a week. He became erect and reached orgasm although this was not particularly satisfying and did not increase sexual self-confidence.

When Karen mentioned the possibility of separation, James panicked. He thought the problem centered on impotence, so he consulted a urologist and planned to get a penile prosthesis. This enraged Karen. All her resentments exploded and she told James "you think with your penis." The last thing Karen wanted was an artificially constructed erection defining her sex life. James was so shaken that he agreed to see a therapist specializing in marital and sexual therapy, something they should have done twenty years before.

Motivation for change is the most important factor in successful therapy. Karen was motivated to rebuild self-esteem and James was motivated to maintain the marriage. The first therapeutic task was to clarify the issues so they could work together as a respectful, caring team. Karen needed to stop feeling blamed and guilty about the rape incident. James apologized for his insensitivity, which had made a traumatic incident more victimizing. Karen had to see James as her intimate friend, and to value a range of affectionate, sensual, and sexual experiences. James had to stop pretending, acknowledge marital problems and take responsibility for his role in the misunderstandings and miscommunications. He had to realize sex was more than erection and intercourse. Sexuality is primarily about sharing touch and intimacy.

Sex therapy facilitates rethinking the role of marital sexuality and experiencing new ways of being sexual. The emphasis is on being an intimate couple, nondemand pleasuring, and multiple stimulation.

Karen and James were surprised to learn that each still masturbated. Rather than this being a shameful secret, it was a good prognostic sign because each spouse still had desire and the capacity for arousal and orgasm. They did a writing exercise involving the rape incident with the intent of reducing stigma and blaming. James apologized for blaming Karen, and described feelings of sadness, confusion, anger, and blaming of self that surrounded the incident and its aftermath. His disclosure made Karen feel closer to him.

The goal was not to return to automatic and autonomous erections, but to experience sexuality as a giving and receiving of pleasure which included, but was not limited to, intercourse. Their sexual relationship was variable, but more intimate and satisfying. They accepted that not all touching would culminate in intercourse.

As Karen and James revitalized their sexual relationship, it promoted marital satisfaction and increased self-esteem. They felt better as people and were satisfied with the decision to remain a married couple.

WHEN THE DECISION IS TO DIVORCE

Some marriages cannot be revitalized. For these couples, remaining married is a negation of self-esteem. Each individual and couple must make a decision based on their values, situation, and family factors. When the decision is to divorce, the person needs to reach out for all the support and self-esteem she can. She is likely to experience two or more difficult years as a single-again person coping with financial, psychological, parental, sexual and practical issues. Those who advocate staying married no matter what claim that divorce is a sign of weakness, or "giving up." In truth, having the courage to divorce is the most difficult, and yet the best thing, some people can do for themselves and their children.

One of the difficulties in writing a self-help psychology book is that no single answer fits all people. For some, the wise and courageous decision is to revitalize the marriage and rebuild self-esteem. For others, it is to confront the fact that this marriage is not viable and to rebuild self-esteem as a single-again person.

You must take responsibility for your decision. If you decide that the marriage subverts self-esteem and is not in your best interest, we applaud your courage to confront this reality and move toward divorce. Divorce is a symbol that this marriage has failed. It is not a sign of personal failure.

Divorce does not mean relinquishing rights or responsibilities toward children. It is important to reassure children that you will continue to be a responsible, caring parent, that the marital problem is an adult one, not caused by children. Nor can the child solve it; children mistakenly believe that if they are especially good or especially bad, they can make parents stay married or get back together. The divorce process impacts children of one or thirty-one years old. Each parent must help the children accept the reality, and their feelings of sadness, confusion, anger, or relief. Parents act in the best interests of their children and themselves if they coparent in a respectful manner without attacking or denigrating the ex-spouse. Maintain emotional distance from the personal, emotional, and sexual life of the ex-spouse. Deal with each other about parental, not personal, issues.

The crucial challenge is to rebuild self-esteem. An unhealthy marriage has a negative impact on self-esteem, although separation and divorce puts self-esteem under further stress. Divorce is a painful process, but you will survive. Leaving a destructive marriage is the right decision. If after careful consideration you have decided that staying married is not healthy, don't engage in "if only" thinking or feel guilty. Use your resources to restore self-esteem, parent your children, and get on with the next chapter of your life.

TEN

Spouse Abuse

How long can or should you tolerate being physically abused in a marriage? The traditional answer was that as long as the abuse wasn't too bad and there were positive elements such as a house, two parents for the children, and financial security, it was tolerable. The feminist view is that once is one time too many—it's time to get out. Can you maintain self-esteem in an abusive marriage? Our answer is that a marriage in which spouse or child abuse continues is not viable. It is the lowered self-esteem of the abused spouse that causes her to feel trapped, able neither to break the abusive pattern nor leave the marriage.

How many marriages experience an incident of physical abuse? If you define physical abuse broadly, to include hitting, spitting, slapping, and pushing, the best estimate is that there has been at least one incident of abuse in over half of marriages. This is a compelling and disturbing statistic. A foundation for self-esteem is a sense of physical safety. When this is at risk, the person's sense of self is unsettled. Middle-class life is based on a sense of physical security and safety. Yet domestic violence, including incidents of child abuse, is endemic in our supposedly middle-class society. When spouse abuse is defined more narrowly, involving weapons, sufficient force to cause noticeable bruising, blood, or a broken limb, the numbers decline significantly, but are still unconscionably high. Approximately fifteen percent of couples have experienced at least one such incident.

There are many varieties of spouse abuse, but they can arbitrarily be divided into two categories. The first is battering. The male consciously uses abuse to dominate and control his spouse and keep her subservient. The violence is planned and instrumental. Suggestions in this chapter are not appropriate for these couples. The treatment of choice is police intervention and separation. The second, and much more common pattern, is that under conditions of stress and frustration the verbal argument accelerates to spitting, hitting, pushing, and, if it continues, more severe forms of physical abuse. Incidents occur as the argument spins out of control, anger accelerates to physical abuse. Neither type of spouse abuse is acceptable, but the second category has a better prognosis for change. These couples have the potential to revitalize their marital bond under conditions of abstaining from violence.

We as a culture, as well as individual couples, need to commit ourselves to eliminating spouse abuse. Rationalizations and justifications for physical violence and coercion have no validity. Spouse abuse is never acceptable in marriage.

BLAME OR RESPONSIBILITY

Who is responsible for spouse abuse? In the typical pattern, both the woman and man engage in verbal putdowns, threats, slapping, and hitting. In most couples, it is the man who accelerates the violence and causes greater physical harm. The husband is the perpetrator and the wife is bruised and beaten. One of the scariest statistics is that among women who are murdered the killer is a spouse, ex-spouse, or boyfriend over forty percent of the time. Males are victims of murder much more than females, but that such a large percentage of murders involve a man with whom the woman was previously intimate is shocking and frightening.

The past approach to spouse abuse placed blame on the woman. She made him mad because of something she did or didn't do and had to take the consequence—a beating. Even more demeaning, she had to ensure that the incident wasn't repeated by being a "good girl" and not causing any upset. In response to this societal message, the feminist movement rebelled, and labeled spouse abuse the natural outcome of culturally inappropriate training about female-male roles. Spouse abuse was viewed as criminal behavior that males perpetrated against females. Women's shelters were established with services to help a woman leave her abusive husband. Police and prosecutors were urged to view spouse abuse as a crime and be advocates for the woman's rights. All men were labeled as potential abusers, rapists, and murderers. A third approach is "family systems theory," which attempts to break the guilt/blame cycle by assigning blame to the family system and its norms. This gets away from the "bad guy-poor woman" syndrome and provides a more comprehensive understanding of the abuse cycle, pointing out that the man and woman each play a role in maintaining an abusive system. Like alcoholism, violence is viewed as a family pathology.

Human behavior is multidimensional and has many sources. For specific couples almost any explanation can have some validity. However, each system of approach has major shortcomings, especially in helping people make decisions about how to intervene when spouse abuse occurs. The first theory is totally unacceptable. It blames the victim, a common trap in our society. Women are held responsible for their husband's behavior, and further burdened by guilt, blame, and low self-esteem. The man is allowed to deny or minimize the violence. He is not confronted with the unacceptability of the abusive behavior and his responsibility for it. Feminist theory is most helpful with a battered woman who needs to build self-esteem and use community resources to help her leave a fatally flawed marriage. For most couples, feminist theory is too simplistic—it is all the male's fault, he's a bad guy because the culture made him that way. Both the man and the woman need to take responsibility for their behavior and change in ways that end the abusive cycle and build self-esteem. These marriages can be revitalized, but only if the violence ends. Family systems theory is so committed to not blaming that it ignores the intimidation caused by the abusive cycle. The person who is stronger and can cause more damage (almost always the male) has to be held accountable for his behavior. The perpetrator needs to be confronted with the fact that the ultimate responsibility for the violence is his.

We believe each person must be committed to a nonviolent marriage. We agree with the view that the "good woman-bad man" conceptualization is not helpful. Both spouses need to be aware of their role in perpetuating the cycle of abuse. Both need to commit themselves to doing what is necessary to halt the cycle. The perpetrator has to be confronted with the reality that no amount of verbal hassle or frustration justifies use of physical force. This includes pushing, slapping, hitting, spitting, kicking, and marital rape, as well as the more physically dangerous forms of battering. The ultimate responsibility for abuse lies with the perpetrator, not the victim. This needs to be clearly stated and understood by all concerned.

Cindi and John. Growing up in a family of origin where there was violence makes it more likely that there will be violence in your marriage. It is not predestined, but is a trap that is easy to fall into and must be carefully monitored.

Cindi vividly remembers seeing her parents fight when she was four. She was both shocked and fascinated, and tried to step between them. She remembers her father shouting at the top of his lungs for her to get out of the way and her mother rushing at him, pushing her fists against his chest. As Cindi grew older, the fights lost their fascination, and feelings of shame and embarrassment predominated. She came to think of her father as powerful and frightening and her mother as emotional and out of control. She switched back and forth as to who she blamed.

Cindi was determined to leave home as soon as possible and marry someone altogether different from her father. John came into her life when she was eighteen, and they married six months later. Cindi was two months pregnant with Crystal. John was twenty-two, recently discharged from the service. He was a quiet-spoken young man, very different from her loud father.

John's father had left the family when John was eight, and he and his sisters were raised by their mother. As with many female-headed families, they were on the edge of poverty. During high school John valued work more than academics, although he did complete his degree. He loved the freedom of the navy and had considered a navy career, deciding against it because he did not like the long tours of duty at sea. Cindi was John's first long-term girlfriend and he enjoyed the companionship and sex. When he learned she was pregnant, he was ready to "do the right thing" and get married. Cindi was excited about marrying as nice and stable a guy as John and thrilled by the idea of starting a family. She would love the child, have a happy marriage, and her family of creation would be completely different from her family of origin.

John and Cindi might have been a successful couple if they had met four years later and given their marriage two years to establish a strong bond before having a child. However, like one in four couples, they were pregnant. This cheats them of the time to develop communication skills, get accustomed to living together, and enjoy couple time.

The sense of disillusionment set in even before the baby was born. Cindi wanted to spend more time together; John felt he needed the time after his construction job to do things with the guys. He wanted an apprenticeship so he could learn a skilled trade. Cindi had friends and activities and didn't view herself as a dependent person, but was disappointed in how difficult it was to get John to discuss personal and emotional issues. John's lack of involvement with their daughter was particularly distressing. He had never been around babies and felt out of his element. Instead of asking for Cindi's help and increasing comfort and skill, he took the easy way out and avoided the whole baby experience. Cindi began losing respect for John, and with lack of respect the marital fabric began to unwind.

Extramarital affairs are listed as a major cause of spouse abuse, but more often an affair is the straw that breaks the camel's back. The conditions for marital alienation are in place before it happens. Contrary to popular belief, affairs do not occur with greatest frequency after many years of marriage, but are most likely during the first three years. Part of the reason is high opportunity. Friends and people you work with are single or divorced, and when you are not getting attention from a spouse, the attention from another person is particularly inviting.

Cindi was shocked to wake up one morning and find herself twenty-one, in an alienated marriage, with a child and a lover. This was not how she imagined things would be at sixteen when she vowed to have an altogether different life from her parents. Affairs eventually come to light, often in an explosive and humiliating manner. John had two or three one-night stands, but when he heard Cindi had a lover, the double standard mentality kicked in. As the betrayed husband, he felt a need to reassert his dignity, and used physical means to do so. This is a common (although indefensible) male trap, asserting masculinity through spousal violence. The shouting, shoving incident culminated with John hitting Cindi on the back with a chair. This is a common pattern: both people are involved in yelling, hitting, and pushing, but when the violence accelerates it is the woman who is more damaged and intimidated.

Few couples have only one violent incident; the pattern is a gradually accelerating sequence of incidents. Cindi had seen this in her family of origin and did not intend to allow it to happen in her life. She did what we strongly recommend in dealing with the initial incident of violence. She called the police and pressed charges. This forces the couple to confront the reality of spouse abuse rather than denying or minimizing it. John was put on notice that he could not get away with hitting or intimidating.

Some couples use the shock effect of the abusive incident and/or police intervention to seek marriage therapy and begin to develop a nonabusive marriage. For Cindi and John there was not enough strength in the marital bond. John continued his avoidance by leaving the house. Cindi was sad, but realized that this was not a viable marriage and accepted the fact that she would be divorced at twenty-two. She was aware that John would not financially support their daughter. Although it would be hard, Cindi knew she would be better off being single than in an abusive marriage. She terminated this marriage with her self-esteem intact, and felt deserving of a second marriage that would be nonviolent.

COUPLES WHO BECOME TRAPPED IN AN ABUSIVE CYCLE

Few women are as decisive as Cindi. Most couples have been in abusive relationships for five years or longer. It's not uncommon to hear of couples who have lived thirty or more years with spouse abuse. The earlier the abuse is confronted, the more likely that it can be reversed and the marriage rebuilt. Where abuse is a chronic problem, the marital bond is so burdened by anger and resentment that it is difficult to revitalize.

Spouse abuse is closely related to alcohol and drug abuse. Abusive incidents are most likely to occur when alcohol is involved. There is a growing body of research and clinical evidence that the male drinks so he can let go and be violent. In other words, alcohol provides an excuse to be physically abusive. Stopping drinking isn't enough; spouse abuse must be confronted. Alcoholism and spouse abuse are similar in that confronting the problem early is preferable, but it's never too late to stop. In Barry's practice, the couple with the longest history that he successfully treated were in their seventies and had had an abusive marriage for forty-one years.

A pattern is established: after a violent incident the perpetrator vows it will never happen again and is genuinely remorseful (although secretly he blames the incident on his wife). There is a honeymoon period where they not only get along, but have special experiences like taking a vacation, buying new furniture, or making plans to move or better their lives. When they must confront difficult issues there is a renewed period of tension and alienation accompanied by drinking, threats, and fears. This can include verbal clashes and lower level physical incidents like throwing things, spanking children, spitting, or pushing. This is followed by a full-blown incident of physical abuse. For many couples it is a single incident, but for most it is a series of incidents that seem to build inevitably to a crescendo. Physical incidents increase in intensity and danger—from a single punch to a series of punches, from threatening with a knife to cutting with a knife, from a bruise on the arm to a broken arm. There is a sense of being out of control and endangered. The victim feels helpless, degraded, and increasingly frightened and hopeless. The perpetrator denies the seriousness of the violence and blames the cycle on the partner, alcohol, or the provocation. He says he's sorry, *but* denies personal responsibility for the violence. He claims that as long as there are no problems and the spouse doesn't provoke him it will never happen again.

A particularly poisonous cycle is the couple who use sex to make up after a violent incident. It's as if the violence were foreplay for a sexual coming together. The passion of sex is supposed to sweep away the abusive incident. One of our strongest recommendations is not to be sexual for at least forty-eight hours after a violent incident. Sex and violence need to be completely separated. This includes not allowing any pushing, roughness, threats, or coercion during sex. The violence-sex cycle is particularly destructive.

Exercise One: Assessment of Violence in Marriage

This is a difficult, but crucially important, exercise. Each spouse does the assessment independently. Each needs to confront denial and look with as much objectivity and detail as possible at the reality of marital violence. You'll need a pen and two pieces of paper. On the first page, list as many physically abusive incidents as you can remember, starting with the most destructive and frightening. Especially note whether weapons (knives, chains, belts) were used, whether alcohol or drugs were involved, places and times of incidents, whether alone or in front of people, whether the violence was one-way or reciprocal. What are the patterns? Is it always late at night, after drinking; does it only happen when you are alone at home? Try to remember the consequences of the abuse incidents. Were the police called; did you not talk for days after; were there threats or promises; did you make up by having sex; did you seek therapy from a psychologist or minister? Did any intervention work and for how long? If the abuse did stop, what started it again and what were the consequences?

On the second piece of paper, list abusive incidents in the past six months in as detailed a manner as possible. Be especially aware of trends—are incidents increasing in frequency or intensity; what happens with promises and threats; are incidents unpredictable or have they become almost ritualistic; does sex serve to reinforce the violence cycle; have there been attempts to intervene and break the pattern in the past six months? How motivated are you to stop the abusive cycle?

Once you have completed this exercise, keep a copy for yourself and give a copy to your spouse. There is a strong urge to be argumentative about this data. The perpetrator tries to minimize the problem, and the spouse demands repentance and restitution for all past incidents. If the couple allow themselves to be sidetracked by arguing about details, the value of the exercise is negated. This exercise is to increase awareness and confront denial. Does this marriage have a problem of spouse abuse? Whether the problem is mild, moderate, or severe, and what to do about prior incidents are secondary issues. Don't be distracted from the main task: recognizing spouse abuse and addressing it as a couple problem. Couples find it extremely difficult to break a cycle of spouse abuse without outside intervention. The need is for professional therapy involving both people.

INTERVENTIONS FOR SPOUSE ABUSE

Spouse abuse therapy is a sub-specialty of marriage therapy. It is a new field with relatively few people trained in these specialized skills. It is important to choose a therapist who is competent and with whom you feel rapport. Be sure the therapist respects you and your goals. The ideology of some therapists (especially pastoral counselors) is that a marriage must be preserved no matter what. Others (especially feminist therapists) believe that when there is spouse abuse the woman must be protected and the marriage ended. Some therapists work with couples. Other therapists conduct couples groups; some clinicians utilize therapy groups for males and therapy groups for females. There are structured programs focusing specifically on spouse abuse, which is our preferred treatment intervention.

The most important factor is to stop the violence. If your goal is to revitalize the marriage, this needs to be understood and respected by the therapist. Be aware that, unless the spouse abuse stops, there is no hope for the marriage. Stopping the violence doesn't guarantee that the marriage can be revitalized. Resentment and anger may overwhelm feelings of respect, trust, and intimacy. Males are loath to confront spouse abuse because of the fear that if they give up their power and intimidation, they will be abandoned. We cannot reassure males that this won't happen. Divorce is the outcome for many couples with a history of spouse abuse. Yet, if the male is to regain self-respect, he has to feel that his spouse stays married not because of fear and intimidation but because of renewed respect, trust, and intimacy. Threatening homicide or suicide if he senses abandonment will not save the marriage, but further lowers self-esteem and can lead to tragic consequences.

An underlying fear is that the person can't survive without the spouse. Not only does each person survive, but there can be renewed self-esteem. Divorce is a difficult and painful process, but in the long run it's better than being trapped in an abusive marriage.

Exercise Two: The Agreement About Nonviolence

We suggest that this agreement be carefully talked out and written down and that each person have a readily accessible copy. It would best be developed in consultation with a therapist. If you choose to make an agreement on your own, be sure it's in the context of a rational discussion where there are neither alcohol, threats, nor intimidation. Don't make an agreement unless it meets each person's needs as well as promoting the marriage, and has a good chance of success. There must be clear negative contingencies if the agreement is broken.

Look at the data from the first exercise and identify the worst incident that occurred (it could be a broken arm, a threat with a weapon, hitting with closed fists). This is the "base" incident. Agree that if this is repeated or something worse happens, the police will immediately be called, charges will be pressed, and both persons agree that the marriage will be terminated. The couple cannot accelerate the violence. If this is to be a safe house with the possibility of revitalizing the marriage you need to move forward. Repeating the "base" incident is a disastrous regression and will result in terminating the marriage.

Spell out the types of spouse abuse incidents to which you are vulnerable. Be as specific as possible. It is not enough to say "when we're angry we push and shove." Be honest about exactly what happens—"I slap him on the cheek," "I push against her with two open palms," "When drinking I chase her around the house," "I grab a knife and say if he comes a step closer, I'll stab him." List the specific incidents each person is vulnerable to acting out if he or she loses control. It is crucial to recognize it is the individual's responsibility to prevent acting out a violent incident. Your spouse cannot force you to act out. The responsibility for a violent incident lies with the perpetrator.

Each person lists what he or she can do to prevent the violent incident. Be as clear and specific as possible. Say, "When I feel I'm starting to get out of control, I will call a time-out and leave the house for an hour;" "I will go into the den and reread my agreement to stop spouse abuse incidents;" "I will keep all weapons locked in a special drawer in the garage." Make requests to defuse the situation. Even if the spouse doesn't keep her end of the agreement, it is still your responsibility to keep your part. A violent incident is like a snowball rolling downhill. The earlier in the cycle you intervene, the better chance to avoid a violent incident.

If the situation gets out of control and violence appears imminent, either partner can signal a "time-out," which is immediately implemented without discussion or argument. Time-out refers to breaking contact, going to separate rooms, and having at least a half-hour cooling-off period to stop the escalating cycle of anger. After the half-hour, the person who called it is responsible to either resume the conversation in a rational way, or, if she feels the situation is too tense or volatile, to say that and reinitiate the discussion within twenty-four hours. This is to insure a time-out is not used as a manipulation to avoid dealing with the issue.

A final element is having clear negative contingencies if the agreement is broken and there is an incident. Each type of incident has a specific negative contingency. For example, a pushing incident would result in the perpetrator having to clean the bathrooms for the next month, a hitting-in-the-face incident would result in his/her leaving the house and having to sleep at a friend's or relative's for three nights (and disclosing what happened), and use of a weapon or physical injury (drawing blood or breaking a limb) would result in calling the police and pressing charges. Rather than viewing these as threats, each person needs to accept the contingencies as a statement that spouse abuse will not be tolerated. This agreement is an important resource in breaking the abuse cycle. A violation of the agreement results in a specific negative contingency. If these agreements are not honored, the marriage cannot continue. The base of self-esteem and marriage is a sense of security and trust.

Alice and Alan. Not all perpetrators of domestic violence are men. When Alice was drunk, she threw things at Alan and hit and pushed him. When Alan saw that she was starting to drink to excess and become agitated, he made sure the children were out of harm's way. The children heard but did not witness the fights. Alan's strategy was to fend off Alice's blows, but not strike back. When she was drunk and out of control he could not reason with her, but stayed in the same room to be sure she did not harm herself or the house. He was afraid of her suffocating in her own vomit or setting the house on fire when she discarded cigarettes or matches. Two years before Alan had had a consultation with an alcoholism counselor who said he was being a "passive victim." Alan felt misunderstood and put down and did not return for counseling. He regularly attended Al-Anon meetings where he felt supported. Alan believed that as long as Alice drank, the spouse abuse incidents would continue. Alice denied both the alcoholism and spouse abuse, saying Alan was at fault for being weak and not making enough money. Alice and Alan have a sad marriage where the likelihood of change is minimal because neither spouse directly addresses the problems of alcoholism and spouse abuse.

A PERSONAL NOTE

On our third date we took a romantic moonlight swim and had our first discussion about family violence. Both Barry and Emily came from families of origin in which there was anger, intimidation, and spouse abuse. In Emily's family both her mother and father engaged in hitting and pushing; since her mother was on crutches she was more heavily damaged. In Barry's family the abuse was one-way; his father ruled by threats and intimidation, and when he did lose control he could be quite frightening. Emily's parents were not physically violent with her, but Barry's father was, with him and his sister.

We talked about our families after the swim. Both of us were committed to not repeating the pattern of violence and spouse abuse in our lives and marriage. Emily made it clear that she would not tolerate physical abuse. Barry said that if the marriage degenerated into violence he would leave. We talked more the next day. Our first couple agreement was that there would be no physical violence between us. This might not seem very romantic for a young couple (in fact, our courtship was quite romantic and special), but we needed to be clear that this would be a nonabusive relationship. To be viable and worthwhile our marriage needed as its base a sense of respect and trust which would be broken if there were violence. We would not stay married if our relationship became violent or abusive. We have been married twenty-five years and are proud to have honored our agreement.

GUIDELINES FOR A NONVIOLENT MARRIAGE

The goal of a spouse abuse program is the complete cessation of family violence. This is crucial for the self-esteem of each spouse, the base for revitalizing the marital bond, and in the best interest of children. It is a difficult task, which is why we suggest professional therapy and a support group. Understanding that the marriage will end if you cannot succeed in breaking the abuse cycle serves to increase motivation. This should not be a threat or manipulation. What happens with many couples is that leaving becomes a hollow threat used in the middle of an altercation, believed by neither spouse. Threats of divorce serve to accelerate an incident.

In halting spouse abuse and revitalizing the marital bond,

there are several issues that need to be confronted. The longer the history of abuse and the more intimidating and physically damaging, the more difficult the task and the greater the need for therapy and a support group. Many couples report abusive incidents began premaritally, that the relationship has never been free of violence. The longer the abuse, the greater the resentment and the lower the intimacy. The greater the marital discord, with more areas of dissatisfaction, the poorer the prognosis. Couples with low self-esteem who are in conflict about money, sex, and children, and stay together for practical reasons or fear of being alone, will have an extremely difficult struggle in rebuilding a marital bond. Conversely, couples with a history of a nonabusive relationship, who have personal and couple strengths, incidents limited in time and intensity, and who are committed to a nonviolent marriage, have a greater chance of success (especially with therapy).

One thing couples do have on their side is that frequency and intensity of physical aggression decreases with age. Twenty to thirty is the age where there is most couple violence. For some couples, the pattern of verbal and physical abuse becomes a powerful, overlearned habit and is as much a part of their lives as their morning cup of coffee. These couples need to be awakened to the destructiveness of spouse abuse. Violence not only tears at the marital bond, but is harmful to the entire family. Children deserve to grow up in a home where there is security and safety. When motivated, couples can learn to communicate, discuss alternatives, solve problems, and conduct their relationships in a nonabusive manner.

THE BATTERED WOMAN SYNDROME

There are couples who are inappropriate for the guidelines and exercises we've presented. The best example is people caught in the "battered woman syndrome." This is one of the most severe forms of spouse abuse, typified by episodes of violence in which the man uses physical abuse to control.

He beats his wife so severely that she goes to an emergency room or a battered woman's shelter. When they are separated, the man threatens suicide or homicide and the woman feels she cannot live without him. The core of her self-esteem is saving her husband and marriage. This is a high-risk, destructive, and symbiotic dependency relationship. These couples definitely need professional therapy. The usual intervention is to have them live apart and each to be seen in individual or group psychotherapy to build self-esteem. Most of these marriages will end in divorce. To create a successful, nonviolent marriage where there is a history of wife-battering is extremely difficult. This is the type of marriage that often needs a frightening incident and police intervention to force a separation.

CLOSING THOUGHTS

Spouse abuse and family violence is very complex and emotionally charged. It can range from verbal harassment and humiliation to pushing and slapping to battering and in extreme cases to death. In the past, spouse abuse was a topic shrouded in secrecy and silence, with a strong inclination to blame the victim. As denial has been confronted, and with increased public awareness, there is a growing body of theoretical and clinical work that has generated much heat but less light. Intervention programs for couples are still in their infancy. Services range through battered women's shelters, support groups, couples therapy, groups for batterers, couple therapy groups, and structured group programs for spouse abuse (the latter is our recommended intervention).

We believe spouse abuse is caused by and contributes to low self-esteem for both individuals. Spouse abuse tears at the fabric of the marriage, decimating respect, trust, and intimacy. Growing up in a family where there are threats and violence is destructive for children. Children who grow up in abusive families are more likely to be abusive in their marriages and with their children. Couples need to confront and change this pattern for the sake of their children as well as themselves. Both spouses and children deserve to live in a safe environment.

We strongly recommend professional therapy in dealing with spouse abuse. Be sure to choose a therapist with competence in this area who will listen to your needs and goals rather than conduct therapy based on personal ideology. Unless the perpetrator takes personal responsibility and is committed to having a nonabusive marriage, the couple cannot break the violence cycle. If this is to be a viable marriage, the couple has to work together to revitalize the marital bond. If the spouse abuse cycle continues, self-esteem cannot grow and the marriage is not worth preserving. Although divorce is difficult and painful, it is healthier than staying in an abusive marriage.

ELEVEN

Stress and Crisis

An important function of marriage is as a buffer and support through times of stress and crisis. What happens when it is the marriage itself that causes stress? People look to the spouse for support, but what if he's your worst critic? We will consider stress and crises that do not involve the marital bond and then those caused by the marriage.

JOB AND CAREER STRESSES

Stress is most commonly caused by job or career problems. Especially stressful is the experience of being laid off or fired. Next to decisions about whom to marry and whether to have children, occupational choices are the most important in how you organize your life. Many people neither plan nor choose a career but "happen into" a job. They face a crisis when they find themselves bored or burned out, or the economy changes and they lose the job.

A job need not dominate self-esteem. Whether doing well or badly, career should not be more than one-third of self-esteem. In the middle of a job crisis, that's a perspective hard to maintain. Negative feedback or rejection is never easy. Being fired affects not just feelings. You worry about paying the mortgage, your ability to get another job, your competence, and how to explain this to colleagues, and friends, and on a job application. Your spouse cannot change the reality, but can reinforce your value and remind you that she loves and respects you. She can help put the job crisis in perspective and together you will weather the disruption.

Self-help books and career consultants urge the person to view the job crisis as a career opportunity. It's a chance to make a dramatic life change—go back to school, start your own business, switch careers. Although this can and does happen, these upbeat stories are the exception rather than the rule. Most people do not have the money, time, or luxury to change careers. The primary goal is to be reemployed. One role of the spouse is to alleviate feelings of desperation so that the next job choice is better thought out and likely to be successful. Realistically, it is easier to change jobs when you have a job. People make better decisions, including career decisions, when not in crisis.

The spouse can play a vital role, especially when the person needs to be confronted with a difficult reality. Confrontation works best in the context of a respectful, trusting, and caring relationship. The confrontation is not a personal attack, but focuses on specific problem behavior. For example, the job crisis might have been caused by drinking, being late, cheating on expense reports, overpromising, anger at a colleague, ignoring warning signs of impending trouble, not doing work in a timely fashion, depending on past achievements, refusing to take a training program to upgrade skills. The spouse is not being kind by colluding to deny his role in the job crisis. He can go to a bar and the bartender will reinforce his explanation that it's the system's fault, the economy, a boss who is out to get him, the envy of fellow workers. A true friend and supporter will reinforce his worth while helping him confront what went wrong and learn from his mistakes. He cannot expect the spouse to be his therapist or rescuer, but can expect her to be a trusted, good friend who will help him confront reality as well as support him.

A particular trap is to pretend that everything is okay and

to deny dealing with reality. Barry has clients who lose jobs and tell colleagues they are free-lancing, consulting, or starting their own business, when in reality they feel embarrassed and are hiding. The worst mistake a spouse makes is to help the coverup. A crucial element in psychological well-being is dealing with reality rather than pretending. Deal straightforwardly, don't get involved in covering up. Don't facilitate your spouse living in a pretend world. The concept of the spouse as an enabler is true not only of job problems, but alcoholism, gambling, eating disorders, financial irresponsibility, and other dysfunctional behavior. You are not being loving by helping him deny or minimize a problem.

Dealing with a job crisis is a two-step process. The first step is to confront the reality of the job loss. Mobilize yourself by beginning the job hunting process, monitor expenses, apply for unemployment benefits. Stay with this difficult process until you find a reasonable job. A second step is to examine your career and either stay in the same field and improve your skills and marketability—the most common alternative—or make concrete plans for a successful career change. People stay in the same field in part because they are not willing to take a pay cut and pay their dues to learn a new field. It is possible to switch careers during a job crisis, but it's easier if you have a job.

There are people who need the impetus of a crisis to get them to take a career risk. For example, Barry had a client who had been in sales for over eight years. A sales career requires the person to put herself on the line continually and not be reactive to rejection. This woman was moderately successful in sales, but found it personally unsatisfying because she couldn't tolerate rejection and became depressed when there was a sales downturn. It wasn't until the company went bankrupt that she mustered the courage to switch careers to property management, an occupation that better matched her skills and personality.

A job crisis is difficult both for individual self-esteem and the marital bond. Yet it is one of the most predictable of life stressors. The average person will change jobs six times in her life. A sense of competence and achievement, whether as a store manager, accountant, homemaker, or student, is an integral element of self-esteem. When that is strained by a stressful or unsatisfactory job, the problem needs to be addressed rather than allowed to fester. Hating what you do eight hours a day is a drain. There is a tendency to take job frustrations out on the spouse, mostly because she's there. It's unfair, and causes you to ignore the job dissatisfaction that is the source of the problem.

In the past, men worked and women remained at home. The traditional female occupations—teaching, nursing, office work—were less prestigious, and women almost always earned less money than their husbands. This has changed dramatically in the past decade, as women have entered a variety of careers. There are a significant number of women in higher paying and higher status jobs than their spouses. This role reversal needs to be addressed rather than ignored or discounted. Each spouse taking pride in and being rewarded for career accomplishments is healthy. A two-career family is the norm among American couples. However, all changes entail tradeoffs, and one potential trap is spousal competition. When his wife makes more money or has a more prestigious job, the man reacts by questioning his competence and feeling lowered self-esteem. He indirectly expresses hostility through belittling remarks or insisting she be responsible for household chores or take off work if a child is sick. The woman finds it hard to acknowledge and enjoy her success; she worries she'll bruise his ego and lose the marriage. The old rules about husbands, wives, and money were simple and easily understood, but were personally limiting and irrational. Career and money issues are not inherently stressful. If the couple can discuss feelings and perceptions and reach an agreement about financial matters that acknowledges each person's contribution, having a two-career family in which the woman makes more money can be positive, not a source of conflict.

Sylvia and Craig. Sylvia came from an entrepreneurial family where financial success was highly valued. Her father urged Sylvia to get a professional degree so she would be insulated from the downturns of the business market. Her mother encouraged her to pursue medicine, but Sylvia found law more interesting. Sylvia's road to life in law was competitive and full of hurdles—acceptance into a prestigious undergraduate college and the achievement of high grades there, scoring well on the LSAT, being admitted to the "right" law school, making good grades to get a proper placement, passing the bar exam, clerking for a judge, becoming an associate at a prestigious law firm, and, finally, making partner.

In her third year at the firm, Sylvia met Craig, who had graduated fourth in his law school class. Both Craig's parents had been teachers and they had encouraged him to pursue academic excellence and public service. After law school, he worked for a public interest legal foundation and served in state government, and his career goal was to be a judge. Craig came from a loving, cohesive family. Marriage and children were a high value for him. He imagined himself marrying a teacher or a woman involved in social service, so he felt strange about dating Sylvia. It was Sylvia who pursued Craig because she was impressed by what a loving, bright, and kind person he was. She admired his family and desired that type of family for herself.

Combining two careers, marriage, and two sons was more of a challenge than either Sylvia or Craig had bargained for. Nine years after their marriage, Craig was a judge, a high-status but not well-paying job. Sylvia had become a partner, but found the continual pressure to generate new business and billable hours, and the supervision of associates, stressful. She had imagined that once she became a partner the stress would be reduced—instead it increased. Juggling two children and a household was difficult—Sylvia and Craig joked that they needed a "traditional wife." He wanted them to live a lower-key lifestyle, but she said, for tax reasons and their position in the community, that they could afford and should have an elegant house, luxury cars, and overseas vacations. Sylvia earned three times as much as Craig and he acquiesced to her desires.

Craig loved being a judge and writing about legal and social issues. He strove to maintain a balance between work, marriage, and family. His self-esteem and sense of satisfaction remained high. However, Sylvia was becoming increasingly dissatisfied. She enjoyed law less than Craig, felt burned out, did not have the close-knit family she desired (partly because her sons resented her frequent business travel), and worried about the economic health and stability of the firm. A crisis was precipitated when three prominent partners left and took seven associates. Craig was supportive over the next three months as Sylvia tried to stabilize her practice and deal with the firm's turmoil. However, she became increasingly unhappy—she was working harder, enjoying it less, and making less money.

Sylvia blamed Craig for the dilemma, and pressed him to leave his judgeship and increase his income. She said he'd been sponging off her for years, and that it was time he acted like a man and provided more money. Craig was offended, but did not counterattack because he did not want the exchange to spiral into an out-of-control, dirty fight. He suggested that Sylvia change jobs and they get a home equity loan. Craig was not willing to be scapegoated because of Sylvia's career dissatisfaction.

They agreed to discuss career and financial options each Monday night until they came to a resolution. These discussions were difficult because there were both practical dimensions—money and mortgages, and psychological dimensions—career satisfaction, how to organize individual and couple life, whether they could accept living a less extravagant lifestyle in a smaller house. Reluctantly, Sylvia gave up the idea that Craig would be the knight in the children's story and rescue the damsel in distress. She had to make difficult professional decisions and to accept this as her responsibility. They, as a couple, had to make house and lifestyle decisions. Sylvia concluded that the benefits of being a partner outweighed the costs, but she needed to establish a different niche. She did not seek reappointment to the management committee, and focused her energy on rebuilding the practice group. This would mean a reduction in bonuses, but she felt more in control of her hours and the direction of her career. Craig supported this decision, and was extremely helpful in discussing strategy and tactics to successfully implement the changes. They decided to stay in the house and take a home equity loan, but did change some spending habits. They stopped trying to keep up with their rich friends and decided to spend vacations at the beach instead of in Europe, which their sons really appreciated.

THE STRESS OF PERSONAL PROBLEMS

All people have areas of vulnerability that can host a full-blown problem. These include phobias, eating disorders, alcoholism, sexual dysfunction, depression, headaches, chronic pain, parenting burnout, alienation. The best strategy is prevention—the individual is aware of the personal vulnerability and monitors it so he doesn't fall into that trap. For example, a man who is vulnerable to misuse of medications would inform his physician of his potential for abuse, so that medications were prescribed sparingly and in small doses. He would ask his spouse to check his use of over-the-counter or prescription medications once a month to ensure that there was not a pattern of abuse. Awareness of the vulnerability is necessary, but not sufficient. There needs to be an active plan to monitor and prevent the behavior from becoming a major problem.

Although prevention is preferable, most people have to experience the problem before being motivated to change. There is denial or minimization so a problem is not addressed until it's severe. Phobia provides a good example. Fear of flying might begin with discomfort about long plane rides, progress to avoiding planes by driving, then further progress to anticipatory anxiety and the canceling of reservations, and finally to the refusal to fly. The spouse doesn't challenge (to avoid being accused of nagging), and the phobia is neglected. The couple engages in a conspiracy of silence. The problem explodes when there is a need to fly and the phobic person feels pressured and belittled. The spouse is angry and frustrated that the phobia is controlling their lives. The time to address a problem is when it's in a mild to moderate stage. The more the person avoids, the stronger the phobia. Identifying and dealing with the problem instead of denying or avoiding, is crucial. The strategy is to approach the phobic situation gradually so that comfort and confidence increases.

When a problem—whether depression, obesity, obsessive-compulsive behavior, alcohol or drug abuse—has gotten out of control, it is necessary to seek outside intervention rather than trying to change on your own. Seeking therapy is not a sign of weakness or "craziness." It demonstrates good judgment. The likelihood of a successful resolution increases with professional intervention. Addressing a problem, not remaining in denial, boosts self-esteem. It is unusual to experience a total cure of a psychological problem—the phobic person does not switch careers to work for the airlines. However, people do make significant progress in their area of vulnerability so it is no longer an incapacitating problem. Most important, they become aware of coping strategies and techniques to monitor and reduce the problem in the future. Another example is the person who compulsively overspends. He changes money habits and retains only one credit card, with a $1000 limit, so that he is no longer vulnerable to out-of-control spending. As the problem is dealt with, self-esteem increases.

What is the spouse's role? One extreme is to treat the problem as if it's yours, get overly involved, and assume responsibility for change. The other extreme is to be so detached that you are oblivious to the problem and your spouse's psychic pain. Our guideline is to be concerned, supportive, and open to requests for help, but to maintain perspective. It's the spouse's problem, don't make it yours. It's counterproductive to berate the spouse for being depressed and equally counterproductive to become depressed yourself. Be aware and caring, but don't feed the depression by putting the spouse down or trying so hard to rescue her that you stop attending to your own agenda. Don't allow the problem to dominate your life or marriage. In the Al-Anon program for spouses of alcoholics, the central concept is detachment. Don't detach from the person, do detach from the problem behavior. The concept of codependent has been overgeneralized and overused. The essence is that you cannot be totally dependent on another person for self-esteem and personal worth. The addict depends on a substance—alcohol, drugs, food, gambling, sex, work—that controls his life. The codependent is addicted to the spouse and controlled by the spouse's problems.

People need a number of sources for self-esteem. Marriage should never contribute more than one-third; self-esteem cannot depend primarily on the spouse. In healthy marriages, there is a balance of autonomy and intimacy. You care about and support the spouse, but are aware that her problems are not your problems and need not dominate.

Dana and Richard. Dana was twenty-seven, married for two years to twenty-six-year-old Richard. She was very involved in twelve-step programs, belonging to Adult Children of Alcoholics, Overeaters Anonymous, and Spenders Anonymous. Richard supported her desire to manage her life better, but felt her psychological energy was going to twelve-step groups, with little left for the marriage. Richard had a number of obsessive-compulsive behaviors and Dana urged him to join Emotions Anonymous and wanted them to attend the Couples in Recovery group. Richard was skeptical and resistant. The more Dana pushed, the more compulsive Richard became. They were locked into a struggle that was destructive for self-esteem and sapping vitality from the marital bond.

Richard agreed to seek couples therapy. The therapist's focus was to differentiate Dana's problems, Richard's problems, and couple problems. They chose a therapist who was knowledgeable and supportive of twelve-step programs and could help them address individual and couple problems.

Richard's perfectionism and ritualistic behaviors were directly confronted. He kept a diary of obsessive thoughts and compulsive behaviors, and engaged in exercises where he was exposed to anxiety-provoking situations but did not perform the ritualistic, compulsive behaviors. Dana was supportive during this process, and both were gratified to see a gradual, significant decrease in obsessive thoughts and compulsive behaviors. The therapist suggested that Dana focus on one twelve-step program, and she chose Overeaters Anonymous, where she developed a supportive relationship with a sponsor. She made progress managing her eating when she remained focused, rather than feeling scattered among groups with overlapping concerns. Some members challenged Dana's decision. She stated that this was the right decision for her at this time and didn't engage in a defensive argument.

Richard and Dana were learning to take responsibility for their behavior, to support the spouse in the change process without taking over the problem, and to work together in reaching couple agreements. They learned to maintain individuality and engage in activities that reduced stress and provided renewed energy. Richard enjoyed running and tennis. He looked forward to these activities, and they kept him in good physical condition and provided an enjoyable social outlet. Dana's physical outlet was aerobics and her favorite way to feel reenergized was going to dinner with a female friend. Richard and Dana discovered two activities they could do together that were stress-reducing and fun. One was a Sunday hike club—it was excellent exercise and they met interesting couples. The second was a weekend stay at a country inn. This allowed them to get away as a couple, explore a different area, and renew their sexual relationship without overspending on a luxury hotel. When a couple have children, weekends away become even more vital. The most important bond in a family is the husband-wife bond. Taking time to be a couple is good for each person, the marriage, and the family. Richard and Dana had never heard this concept before therapy, but now are converts and encourage friends to try it.

Richard's compulsive behavior and Dana's weight problem were not altogether eliminated. For most people, the ideal of a total cure is unrealistic. What *is* realistic is a gradual change until the problem no longer dominates self-esteem nor is it a major factor in the marriage. Dana gave up her unrealistic weight goal of a hundred twenty pounds and set a viable weight range between a hundred thirty and a hundred thirty-five pounds. She could maintain that weight with a sensible eating and exercise regimen. Richard and the Overeaters Anonymous group supported this. Dana felt in control of her eating and life. She would need to remain aware and monitor weight and exercise, but no longer perceived herself as having an eating disorder.

Richard found compulsive behavior hard to change. The cognitive change from perfectionism to competence was valuable. Keeping data on and reducing ritualistic, compulsive behaviors like checking and counting were successfully implemented. The persistent difficulties involved compulsive habits that were utilitarian, such as cleaning the house and balancing the checkbook. Dana wished he didn't do it to such an extreme, but did appreciate his taking care of those tasks. Richard found it easier to abstain from a compulsive behavior than to try to moderate it, but behaviors like eating, cleaning, and paying bills cannot be abstained from. Dana and Richard acknowledged each other's changes and helped maintain improvements rather than aiming for perfection.

STRESS INVOLVING THE MARRIAGE

Most people would choose an external source of stress rather than internal—for example, being fired from a job rather than experiencing a panic attack. They would prefer a problem they could work on together and support each other to a problem with each other. However, the sad reality is that marriage is a major stressor for a large number of people. In research on stressful life events, separation and divorce is second on the list (only the death of a spouse or child is rated more stressful).

If marital stress and dissatisfaction are problems, you need to face that reality rather than deny it. Pretending that everything is fine or minimizing the problem by saying all couples have troubles won't help. The three major stressors for married couples are problems involving children, money, and sex. If not dealt with, they will weaken or destroy the marital bond.

CHILDREN

Some children are easier to parent than others. In general, stepchildren and blended families are more difficult than nuclear families. Questions of split loyalty, visitation, coparenting arrangements, how involved (especially in discipline) the stepparent should be, the ''my children-your children'' distinction, all add layers of complexity. Children who are physically handicapped, emotionally disturbed, alcohol or drug abusers, or who act out are particularly difficult.

Many parenting problems reflect a conflict between the couple. The conflict often involves a triangle, the child aligned with one parent and the other left out. Each parent takes a stance—one is the disciplinarian, the other the buddy. This often involves a male-female double standard, male children treated differently from female children. The parent who was ignored as a child wants to be sure he attends to his children, while the parent who was sexually abused is hyper-vigilant about the children's safety.

Adult problems and disagreements should not be taken out on children. Children find it upsetting and stressful to be caught in the middle of parental struggles. Such problems can be dealt with by adults communicating and reaching acceptable agreements. Parenting is best done as a respectful, cooperative, caring task. A child who knows he can manipulate by going to one parent for one thing and the other parent for something else is learning a strategy that is not healthy for family relations or the child.

We strongly felt the need to be a team in parenting. Our children complained that we were too much of a united front, and certainly it's possible to be too much of a team and not let individuality show—taking any guideline to an extreme is problematic. It was reassuring to know the spouse would be helpful both practically and emotionally during stressful parenting times.

MONEY

Money is a source of stress for many couples, almost independent of how much is earned. Barry counseled a couple who earned over $600,000 a year but complained that they didn't have enough money to go out to dinner. Couple money management is not a simple matter of income, spending, and accounting. Attitudes, feelings, values, and how money was handled in your family of origin play major roles. We feel like hypocrites writing about this because, of all the content areas of marriage, financial management has given us the most trouble. When we first married we lived on $250 per month and now our income is many times that, but we've had financial difficulties throughout the marriage. It's a chronic problem, but we try not to let it control our lives. Even though we are not a positive model for money management, we would like to offer the following guidelines.

The most important is not to have financial secrets. Be honest with yourselves and each other about what is earned from all sources, and what you spend for everything. Keep an honest budget. Don't fall into the trap of taking dichotomous roles—one is the saver, the other the spender; one worries, the other doesn't care; the one who earns the higher income complains, the other is sneak spending. Negotiating agreements and positively influencing each other is particularly relevant in money management.

The most common financial stress is not having the money necessary to meet needs and desires. It might help to know that's true of over ninety percent of couples—there's never enough money. Rather than blaming and panicking, look at realistic alternatives. Set up a hierarchy of needs (with food, shelter, children, and transportation highest on the list), and save for and sequence other purchases. The most common money management system is "our money, her money, his money." In the "our money" category, funds are set aside for joint responsibilities: mortgage or rent, food, child care, car, insurance, utilities, furniture, health care. The usual procedure is that for a purchase over a certain amount—$200 perhaps—both people need to agree. One person typically takes charge of the checkbook and bill paying, but the other is aware of the financial situation. There is a special fund for vacations, major purchases, retirement, and/or children's education. Whether once a week or every two months, the couple sits down with their budget or computer spreadsheet and reviews the money situation. It never works as well as it could or should, but hopefully it's not too far off target. When there is a problem, don't give up; either cut spending (the preferred alternative) or take a part-time job to temporarily increase income.

We are strong believers in having a clear, concrete money management system (if we could only follow this in our lives), but that's not the whole answer. Money fights involve feelings and perceptions. One spouse feels taken advantage of, the other can't understand why there's no money to buy something important. One spouse comes from a family of origin or first marriage where financial discussions always degenerated into a fight, so money issues are assiduously avoided. For others, the fight over who manages the checkbook is really a fight for control and respect.

One way to break the impasse is to discuss feelings, perceptions, and meanings of money. The emphasis is on sharing information and perceptions, not on decision making or developing a financial management system. Understanding the spouse's history, feelings, and perceptions about making and spending money can clarify conflicts and reduce the tendency to put down or attack. With greater awareness and empathy, it is easier to deal with financial issues.

SEXUALITY ISSUES

One of our favorite points is that when sexuality is working well in a marriage, it's a relatively minor factor. Its major function is to energize the marital bond, and sexuality accounts for fifteen to twenty percent of the marriage. However, when sex is dysfunctional or problematic, it becomes inordinately important—accounting for fifty or even seventy percent of the marriage. A sexual crisis can drain the marriage of good feelings. The three most stressful crises are discovery of an extramarital affair, an infertility problem, or a sexual dysfunction.

Gail and Gary. There is a romanticism and idealism in a college relationship that is special, but sets the couple up for marital and sexual problems in the future. Gail was a sophomore and Gary a junior when they began dating. They were viewed as a "golden couple" by friends because, while other relationships came and went, for a year and half they were a solid couple. This changed three months before Gary's graduation when Gail became infatuated with someone else. She had planned to take her junior year abroad, but allowed Gary to talk her out of it. Her resentment over the lost opportunity festered and was acted out in an affair. Gary felt desperate to get her back. The end of his senior year was dominated by the intense roller-coaster of the relationship. He put his energy into pursuing Gail, and skipped job interviews. They reconciled the week before school ended, but not in time to save their academic records for that semester. This was the beginning of a pattern that stretched across the next ten years—periods of stability intermixed with high-stress crises, with individual plans subordinated to the relationship. Their decision to marry three and a half years later involved more of the same. Wedding plans were on and off three times before they wed. Ideally, marriage is a symbol of a lifelong commitment. For Gail and Gary it was just another step in their struggle to remain a couple.

In the premarital years, sex was a forte. By the time they married, it was problematic. Gail, although easily aroused, found orgasm difficult. Gary had been an early ejaculator, but enjoyed being sexual. He decided unilaterally that for Gail to be orgasmic, he had to last longer. He read about the stop-start technique and used it in an abrupt, mechanical manner, which decreased his pleasure, her pleasure, and couple enjoyment. Gary became angry at Gail for not having orgasm during intercourse, was critical of her body (especially her thighs), and questioned how sexual she really was. Gail became increasingly self-conscious and defensive, which resulted in inhibited sexual desire. This was exacerbated by relationship turmoil, in which sexual coming together was the means to reconcile emotionally, followed by a period of avoidance when sex was disappointing.

They hoped marriage would ensure their commitment and resolve sexual problems. Instead, the excitement didn't even last until the wedding. The honeymoon was filled with conflict about how much sightseeing to do. The only sex they had for those three weeks was the first morning, and that was spoiled by an argument over the amount of movement during intercourse.

The first two years of marriage are vital in establishing a couple style of communicating, expressing negative feelings, reaching agreements, being sexual, and enjoying each other. Gail and Gary were making little progress, but Gail pushed to get pregnant. Her stated reason was that a baby would help bring them together. However, she had a hidden, unspoken agenda. If this marriage did not survive, she wanted a child to demonstrate some worth from her years with Gary. Neither motivation was healthy. Children do not save marriages; they put extra stress on a tenuous relationship. Couples are most likely to break up three months before or three months after the birth of the first child. A child should be planned and wanted, a symbol of commitment and belief in the marital bond.

Stress multiplied when, after six months of trying, they didn't become pregnant. A preliminary fertility workup indicated ovulatory irregularity and problematic sperm motility. The fertility specialist assured them they could become pregnant, but this latest setback caused Gail to become depressed. She felt that dealing with marriage, sexuality, and now fertility problems made life too difficult. At this point, they were referred for couples therapy.

The therapist saw Gail and Gary together, then each alone for a psychological history. In the couple feedback session, the therapist shared her assessment and treatment plan. She viewed their marriage as a pseudo-marriage based on fear and dependency, not intimacy. As individuals and as a couple they would need to make a major, consistent commitment to change. They agreed to a six-month effort to build a viable marital bond.

The first focus was on strengthening individual self-esteem. Gail's depression was addressed, using cognitive therapy techniques. She learned that she was responsible for her well-being, that her self-esteem was not dependent on Gary. Most importantly, she learned to express a full range of emotions, rather than storing up feelings and being swept away by a wave of depression. Gary had to stop blaming, and taking a performance-oriented view of marriage, sex, and fertility. His sexual self-esteem was based on Gail's orgasm and pregnancy, which kept them stuck in the morass. He needed to develop a pleasure-oriented approach to sexuality and involve himself in the process of sharing emotional, sensual, and sexual intimacy. He needed to realize that fertility and masculinity were not connected, and emotionally reinvest himself in the marriage.

The process of rebuilding self-esteem and the marital bond is gradual, with advances, problems, and plateaus. We encourage couples to seek professional therapy rather than trying to make these changes on their own. For Gail and Gary it was a frustrating road; when they made progress in one area, for example Gail's depression, they still had to deal with the continuing stress of the fertility problem.

To increase the likelihood of pregnancy, they utilized an insemination procedure with Gary's sperm. It took four months of twice-a-week visits to the gynecologist's office during the high probability period. Gary masturbated to orgasm into a sterile cup. The sperm was placed by the gynecological nurse directly into Gail's cervix with a syringe. This was awkward and anxiety-provoking, although they felt supported by the empathetic, sensitive nurse. The pregnancy was joyous, but did interfere with sexual progress, especially during the last trimester. Gary reflected on how much he'd learned about himself, sexuality, an intimate marriage, communication, and problem-solving. He just wished the learning had been easier. Gail echoed his feelings, but in a paradoxical way the process helped her come to grips with depression. She could differentiate between depression, which was irrational and self-punishing, and sad or frustrating feelings, which were a natural reaction to stress. Gail came to value sexuality in a way she hadn't previously. She learned to be more comfortable, open, and experimental, and found that it was easier and more fulfilling to be orgasmic with manual stimulation. She no longer apologized to Gary about her sexual style, but invited him to share sexual pleasure and enjoy couple intimacy. The experiences they shared personally, maritally, sexually, and in conceiving a baby were difficult, but built a solid foundation for self-esteem and their marital bond.

CLOSING THOUGHTS

Learning to deal with stress and crisis is integral to self-esteem and an intimate marriage. Rather than avoiding or pretending, difficult issues need to be dealt with in a respectful, caring manner by discussing feelings, perceptions, and alternatives. As Barry advises his clients, "There is seldom a perfect solution, but there are always viable alternatives." Stress and crisis have to be addressed, otherwise they become chronic and severe, lowering self-esteem and robbing the marital bond of vitality. At a minimum you need to regain a sense of equilibrium. Optimally, resolving the crisis will enhance self-esteem, increase confidence in the marriage, and inoculate you against stress in the future.

TWELVE

Revitalizing the Marital Bond

Is this chapter only for couples recovering from a marital crisis? Absolutely not! The major mistake American couples make is neglecting to think about their marriage. You are not the same person who married twelve years ago, nor is your spouse. Expectations and life circumstances are different. As you grow as individuals, your marital relationship can and should change. Marriage cannot rest on its laurels. The optimal strategy is to continuously put time and psychological energy into the relationship in order to maintain an intimate, stable marriage. Unfortunately, that's too idealistic for most couples. What is applicable is the periodic need to assess feelings and attend to the marital bond.

Prevention is the best way to deal with a problem. However, the sad reality for most couples is that they will experience at least one period during which the marital bond becomes weak or badly strained. Let us use a prosaic analogy to car maintenance. The car manual gives you a recommended schedule for maintenance. However, most people take their car to a garage only when they notice a problem or when the problem becomes severe. Mechanics complain that, by the time the car is brought in, there's already a great deal of damage. This is exactly what marital therapists say:

by the time they see the couple, there's a lot of water over the dam. The therapist wishes the couple had come three years before. Over the intervening years, layers of frustration, resentment, and blaming have overshadowed the original problem. Couples usually do not seek help until they are in crisis. The focus is dealing with the crisis and saving the marriage. There is little energy left to revitalize the marital bond or inoculate against future problems.

Respect, trust, and intimacy are the essence of the marital bond. Some couples never build a strong bond, even those married over a decade. An intimate marriage cannot be taken for granted. As time passes and individuals change, respect for the spouse decreases and/or respect for the marriage wanes. Incidents that violate trust devitalize the bond. These include an extramarital affair, ridiculing the spouse in front of family and friends, reneging on an agreement about money or housework, being angry or distracted by a work problem so you ignore family commitments, becoming overly involved with family of origin or a community group, flirting in public, denigrating your spouse's appearance. Emotional intimacy is the glue that holds the marriage together, and neglect is the major cause of its weakening. Special times and feelings become less frequent. People plan, anticipate, and carry out premarital and extramarital affairs, but take marital sex for granted. Frequent and passionate lovemaking gives way to once-a-week sex that becomes mediocre.

If people devoted as little time and energy to maintaining their businesses as couples devote to maintaining their marriages, we would have a bankrupt country. Boredom, routine, and taking each other for granted are major obstacles to marital satisfaction. When life is stable, without problems or crises, it is possible to get by with business as usual. However, personal stress or a family crisis throws an already vulnerable marriage into disarray. Although marriage is supposed to provide support during difficult times, for all too many couples marital dissatisfaction exacerbates other problems. Spouses become each other's worst critics and attack rather than support. The cycle of blaming, anger, and lowered self-esteem that drains the marital bond becomes self-perpetuating.

This is not to imply that healthy marriages do not experience stresses, problems, and crises. The reality is that problems are inherent in the human condition, affecting both self-esteem and marriage. Many problems can be avoided or prevented, but others simply must be dealt with. Couples who work together and survive a crisis are stronger for having successfully confronted it. In the best of cases, the couple not only deal with the crisis but learn to cope so they are inoculated against future crises. The strategy is not to avoid problems, but to deal with them as a team rather than allow the problem to become dominant and controlling. The best prevention strategy is to build and maintain a viable marital bond. Don't take your spouse or marriage for granted.

Kathy and Ted. Kathy was thirty-eight and in her second marriage. She'd been married for three years (this was a first marriage for thirty-nine-year-old Ted). Sex was most satisfying and they felt best about the relationship premaritally. The last three years had been a disappointment, but they'd settled into the marriage and did not expect things to change. Kathy had a fourteen-year-old daughter, Kim, and an eleven-year-old son, Alex, from her first marriage. Kathy and Ted had not planned to have children, but Ted was expressing an interest in having a baby, and as Kathy's biological clock was ticking, she became ambivalent about a last child.

A crisis occurred when fourteen-year-old Kim became pregnant. Kathy felt that she had good communication with her daughter, and so was shocked to discover the pregnancy. She wanted to involve Ted in the crisis, less to deal with Kim than to support herself. Kathy wanted to be helpful, not judgmental. They consulted a female problem-pregnancy counselor to discuss feelings and alternatives. Kathy believed that fourteen was too young to have a child and was extremely supportive, as was Ted, of the decision to have a therapeutic abortion. This type of crisis is an emotional drain, but brought Kathy and Ted closer.

Afterward, Kathy and Ted discussed whether to have a child together and she was relieved when he decided that a baby and the eighteen-year commitment to parenting was not one he wanted. Family planning decisions are among the most difficult a couple make. The financial, practical, and emotional dimensions are enormously complex. Seldom is the decision not to have a child made without ambivalence and regret. Kathy volunteered to have a tubal ligation because she was the one more committed to not having a baby. They were tired of using contraception and worried about dealing with an unwanted pregnancy. One abortion in the family was enough.

This decision freed Ted and Kathy to make other life choices. Kathy had two desires—to buy a house in a more urban neighborhood and enroll in an advanced training program. Ted had a major goal—to return to flying and renew his license so he could take the family on vacation. They couldn't do this all at once, but felt better that they'd established goals. Sharing plans and aspirations enhances the marital bond. They supported each other in reaching individual goals, which, in turn, enhanced their marriage.

Couples need to establish a pattern that provides individual and couple satisfactions on a regular basis. For Kathy this meant a regular exercise program involving aerobic classes and a weekly tennis game. Ted joined her for aerobics much of the time. They used the drive home to catch up on the day's events. Ted's way of relaxing was listening to classical music. After the kids were asleep they would cuddle on the couch, sharing feelings and stories, enjoying each other and the music.

Ted realized the children did not need another father, but he wanted the four of them to function as a cohesive, flexible, blended family. Ted saw his role as that of a favorite uncle. He was particularly pleased by the relationship with Alex. Ted's parents also enjoyed the children, who in turn were glad to have another set of grandparents. Ted coached the boys' soccer team and was an assistant coach of girls' basketball. Kathy was pleased and proud of Ted's involvement. The teams allowed Ted a comfortable way to relate to the children and gave Kathy space and time to pursue her professional training.

One of the thorniest problems involved couple trips. Ted enjoyed planning, anticipating, going on, and reminiscing about vacations. Kathy was concerned about leaving the children, both because she'd miss the contact and was worried that they'd feel left out. There had been a number of bitter arguments about vacations during which Ted called Kathy a "frightened, inhibited stick-in-the-mud!" and Kathy called him a "selfish child who didn't care about anyone except himself." Something that should bring a couple together turned into a dirty-fighting confrontation. They agreed to deal with this issue in a respectful, problem-solving manner. The first guideline was to stop the name calling. Ted shared how important vacations were for his psychological well-being. Instead of fighting what she perceived as his demands, Kathy was able to hear his needs and acknowledge their validity. In turn, Ted accepted Kathy's concern about the children's feelings and needs. He made the suggestion of taking a two-week family vacation, a one-week couple vacation, and getting away for two weekends as a couple. Kathy found this an excellent agreement and promised Ted that in seven years they would have the freedom to travel as a couple.

The quality of the marriage increased as they devoted time and energy to deal with both positive and negative issues. In Ted's family of origin, there had been a very poor marital model of minimal contact and then explosive arguments. He had not planned to marry, but grew tired of the singles scene and the roller-coaster of starting and ending relationships. He married Kathy with relatively low expectations, assuming that the marriage would be stable, but would reduce his personal freedom and not add to life satisfaction. As they worked through the problems of Kim's pregnancy, decided on sterilization, made vacation agreements, and discussed personal feelings and needs, Ted had a renewed feeling of emotional intimacy and a desire to make this an involving, satisfying marriage. When Kathy married Ted she'd hoped for stability, but after her divorce, was wary of investing too much self-esteem in marriage. She had learned a crucially important lesson: you cannot define yourself through another person. She would not fall into this trap with Ted, but was in danger of falling into the opposite trap of a minimally involved marriage. Kathy had to learn to define personal autonomy within the commitment of marital intimacy. This is the crucial balance. She trusted that Ted was willing and able to deal with the good and bad times of marriage. As Kathy's respect and trust grew, so did her emotional investment in the marriage. She could be a caring and loving spouse as long as there was mutual commitment to maintaining an intimate marital bond.

THE BALANCE BETWEEN SELF-ESTEEM AND MARRIAGE

Our theme has been how to create and maintain a positive, reciprocal relationship between self-esteem and marriage. This is not an idealistic, perfectionist goal reached by a tiny minority of people, but a realistic guideline that can be utilized by most. When this balance is disrupted by an individual problem—a phobia, obsessive-compulsive disorder, job crisis, illness, death of a parent—or a problem affecting the marital bond such as an extramarital affair, parenting difficulty, a sexual dysfunction, a pattern of hurtful fights, major disagreement about an important life decision like moving, retirement, or financial problems, the focus is on resolving the problem in a manner that restores self-esteem and revitalizes the marital bond. One is affected by the other. Lowered self-esteem has a negative impact on the marriage. Marital problems and dissatisfactions lower self-esteem.

There need not be a total resolution to restore vitality. Perfect solutions only occur in movies and pop psychology books. He may reduce the frequency and intensity of obsessive-compulsive behavior, but it still needs to be monitored so the behavior doesn't again get out of control. The spouse is still mildly irritated but reinforces the change. Self-esteem is heightened by acknowledging progress. The marital bond will be revitalized by appreciating individual and couple strengths while integrating each person's weaknesses and vulnerabilities without losing respect for the spouse.

In dealing with the aftereffects of an extramarital affair or a disruptive family move, the reality of the problem and feelings needs to be accepted rather than denied. There is no value in pretending it didn't happen or didn't matter. Psychological well-being and self-esteem is based on accepting and dealing with reality. Life is meant to be lived in the present with planning and anticipation of the future, without being controlled by guilt or resentment from the past. The affair occurred and the family did move; these realities cannot be changed—the question is how to integrate them.

Rather than engaging in blame and "if only" thinking, the couple needs to rebuild the trust bond and prevent reoccurrence of affairs. The typical resolution is an up-front agreement not to have affairs. Each spouse identifies a high-risk pattern and designs an early warning system to prevent an affair. The most powerful technique is to tell the spouse *before* it occurs that you are thinking of or tempted to act on an affair. With this system an affair can't just happen or be a secret. You must take responsibility for the behavior and its impact on the marriage.

When a couple moves and there is a negative impact on the children or the spouse's career, or financial problems, or the new house is a lemon, they face difficult adjustment issues. Blaming or threatening does not resolve the problem. Nor does saying "I told you so." The couple needs to adopt a problem-solving approach and look at realistic alternatives. This is not easy, but psychologically is the most productive approach. Continually fighting over the move is not only to remain stuck but to allow for more destructive problems to develop. "When it rains, it pours" goes the saying. The original problem becomes so preoccupying and demoralizing that the family is left vulnerable to new problems. The couple need to work together to deal with problems and begin to build positives in their new environment. If not, they run the risk of their lives and marriage being swamped. Once the situation has returned to an equilibrium, they can review what they've learned in order not to repeat the pattern.

In many marriages, the balance between the individual and couple becomes disrupted. If this is chronic or repeats a family-of-origin pattern, we recommend that the couple seek professional therapy to help them understand and change it. For example, a man is afraid his wife will leave, and deals with this by being hyper-vigilant about her activities, compounding the problem. Continuing the same behavior that caused the problem is a prescription for disaster. The husband's behavior was motivated by fear of abandonment, which he experienced in his family of origin when his mother left for another man, starting a ten-year custody fight. Negative motivation does not promote positive behavior. The first intervention was to build self-esteem and personal worth. As long as he felt he needed her love in order to survive, theirs would be an unhealthy marriage. He had strengths and worth, whether married or not. Once this was understood, he could focus on positive contributions to the marriage. He and his wife needed to build a couple trust bond based on strength, not fear. Marriages work best when each spouse maintains self-esteem.

Keeping the marriage intimate and vital is a joint responsibility, but cannot compensate for individual problems. One cannot cling to the marriage as the only, or even major, source of self-worth. A supportive marriage is of great value during a personal crisis, illness, job loss. However, it is only of value if it helps the person regain equilibrium and move toward healthier coping. Treating the spouse as an emotional cripple will devitalize the marriage. Support means help in coping and getting life on track, not in permanently being in a "one-down" position.

The common trap for men is to focus on career goals at the expense of marriage and family. The common trap for women is to feel so responsible for others (spouse, children, extended family, friends) that they don't attend to personal wants and needs. Men falsely believe that they can postpone attending to marriage and parenting until they've established their careers. The challenge for men is to integrate caring and achievement. Women put off their agendas until everyone is taken care of, and then resent caretaking because it's never their turn. The challenge for women is to integrate independence and nurturance. Psychological well-being for both men and women means maintaining a positive balance as circumstances and roles change. The core element is self-esteem and the core relationship is the marriage.

A PERSONAL NOTE

We wrote this book between our twenty-fourth and twenty-fifth year of marriage. We can identify three periods during which it was necessary to pay special attention to our marital bond. The first occurred after ten years of marriage, when we had an eighteen-month, ultimately unsuccessful, placement of an older child we had planned to adopt. Until that time we were idealistic and optimistic about our ability to do almost anything. We had to deal with sadness and relief, and set new, more realistic goals for our family. The second period was three years later; we had made a very poor decision about a house and were upset about a disappointing book project. The practical problems took four years to solve (culminating in the purchase of a new house), but within a year our marriage was back on track. The third phase was three years ago, when we had to deal with a number of crises, especially a stressful period of adolescence and Emily's mother entering a nursing home. It was humbling to realize that our best intentions and efforts could not remedy very difficult situations. We survived these periods with our self-esteem and marital bond intact. We are entering the "couple again" phase of marriage and are committed to maintaining a strong and intimate bond for the next twenty-five years. We won't be surprised if another difficult period occurs and we'll need to put time and energy into revitalizing our marriage.

The strategy we advocate is to accept the reality of problems, air feelings and perceptions in a non-blaming manner, commit to problem-solving as an emotionally intimate team, and set aside couple time. The latter includes going away for a night or weekend for talk and play and sexual intimacy. Our favorite mode for communication is to take walks and discuss feelings and issues. Emily emphasizes the importance of being together and touching. Barry emphasizes looking at a range of alternatives and reaching agreements. These are complementary approaches and each contributes to dealing with issues and revitalizing the marital bond. A prime guideline is that our marriage is more important than almost any content issue, although we would not make an agreement that would subvert one spouse's self-esteem.

We feel great value from the marriage and are protective of our bond. We celebrate it, rather than consider it work. We take pride in the fact that our marriage is stronger and more satisfying now than in our first ten years.

INOCULATION AGAINST FUTURE CRISES

No one like problems, crises, or marital stress. However, they will occur and can provide an opportunity for growth. This happens if you as a couple work together to resolve the problem and continue past the crisis resolution stage. You need to review what has been learned and what you'll do when similar problems occur. Even more important, discuss how to avoid future problems or have an early warning signal so you deal with the problem before it becomes severe. Try not to be blind-sided by a new problem. Most psychology and marriage self-help books claim problems can be avoided if you follow their advice. We believe issues can be successfully dealt with before they become problems. However, the reality of the human condition and the marital state is that problems occur. Deal with them so they don't control self-esteem and the marriage.

Events that can cause major disruption include a car accident or serious illness. It is not just dealing with the reality of the incident and its aftermath, but the fear about your life. As adolescents and young adults, people take risks with a sense of invulnerability: nothing can happen to me. As you age and experience pain and losses—death of a friend, illness of a parent, your spouse has surgery—you confront the reality of your vulnerability. You've assumed more responsibility, so there's more to lose. An accident or illness has a powerful impact. The spouse deals with practical issues of visiting the hospital, consulting with doctors, getting help with children, worrying about finances and insurance forms, fielding calls from friends and relatives. More draining are the psychological stresses and fears. How serious is this? Is it life-threatening? How will this affect our lives and marriage? Can we survive emotionally after the crisis abates? How will we handle the rehabilitation process? These are not the things people think about when they first marry. The joy and anticipation are great, but shouldn't hide the reality that each individual and couple will go through hard times. The measure of a marriage is its ability to cope with and survive loss and crisis and retain the desire and ability to revitalize the marital bond.

Learning from the crisis inoculates you against painful, out-of-control experiences. In our marriage, we had four simultaneous crises to deal with three years ago. This particularly painful period lasted six months, and the repercussions for two years. We would never want to go through all this again, but the fact that we managed the problems, regained self-esteem, and helped each other, and that our marital bond survived, is a source of pride. This increased self-confidence and confidence in each other. Now, difficulties are easier to deal with because we're confident in our coping strategies and techniques. Inoculation does not mean problems won't occur, but that you have the attitudes and skills to address them.

MARITAL BONDS THAT CANNOT BE REVITALIZED

Not every marital story has a happy ending. When the marital bond is broken, it is very difficult to put back together (even with superglue, it doesn't stick). When the couple stop thinking of themselves as "us" and view the spouse as the enemy or the target of disdain, the marriage has suffered a loss from which it probably cannot recover. Loss of marriage need not mean permanent loss of self-esteem. Marriages that damage one or both spouse's self-esteem should not continue.

Ideally, the marriage would end with a sense of sadness and acceptance, and the couple would separate in a respectful manner and wish each other well. If children are involved, the couple would be responsible and cooperative in parenting. This scenario seldom occurs. Most marriages end explosively, not sadly. He feels rejection and pain, and anger causes him to inflict pain on the ex-spouse. Accusations and putdowns dominate. In the worst-case scenario, the couple play out the *War of the Roses*. It's amazing that someone you once promised to love and cherish can be treated in a hurtful, vindictive manner. Retribution becomes the coin of exchange. Anger and fighting can persist for years. This reaction is a means to deal with feelings of pain and rejection. The emotional basis of anger is hurt. It would be better if the ex-spouse could deal with hurt in a healthier manner. The sad reality is that the marriage is over. The person would do better to get on with his or her life and wish the ex-spouse well. When children are involved, it is easier to coparent if the ex-spouse is doing well.

Most people do not react in a psychologically healthy way to divorce. Over half remain angry ten years afterward. Usually there is a subtle, or not so subtle, conflict between ex-spouses for the loyalty and affection of the children. You compare how well your second marriage is going as opposed to the ex-spouse's, including house and finances. Is anger, competition, or retribution really in your best interest? Wouldn't your self-esteem be better served by focusing on the present and future rather than being dragged down by the divorce and ex-spouse? You can free psychological energy by putting your ex-spouse behind you. Why give the ex-spouse such power to drain your emotions with anger and bitterness? Put the divorce and ex-spouse in perspective, and focus on your present life and self-esteem.

Whether or not the marriage can be revitalized, the most important factor is rebuilding self-esteem. Self-esteem exists part from the marriage and is more important: the person can and will survive a divorce. Realizing this puts the decision of whether the marital bond can be revitalized in a healthier perspective. You have worth as an individual, whether married or divorced. This allows you to decide whether it's possible and worthwhile to revitalize the marital bond.

People motivated by positive factors are more likely to make a good decision than those motivated by fear, anger, or guilt. The decision to remain married is based on the belief that in the future your life and self-esteem will be enhanced by revitalizing the marital bond. Consider the history of the marriage, the needs of children, religious and moral commitments, the influence of extended family, and financial and practical matters. These deserve serious attention, but cannot be decided factors. No amount of money, religious belief, or family pressure can justify staying in a marriage where there is physical or emotional abuse. A marriage that is destructive to self-esteem is not worth maintaining. The individual can rebuild self-esteem as a single-again person. Rather than viewing yourself as a failure because of the divorce, view yourself as strong for having the courage to leave a destructive marriage and be on your own.

THE RECIPROCAL RELATIONSHIP BETWEEN SELF-ESTEEM AND MARRIAGE

Reasons to revitalize the marital bond are that being married raises self-esteem and respect, trust, and intimacy are restored. Is marriage worth it? When a marriage goes well (not perfectly), it meets needs for intimacy and security better than any other relationship. People who feel good about their marriage report higher self-esteem and sense of personal security. Both spouses need to maintain self-esteem. A respectful, trusting, intimate marriage is strong enough to get the couple through good and bad times. Marriage is a basis of their life, but not the sole one.

In writing this book, we had to balance giving positive, understandable guidelines with the complexity and variability present in self-esteem, marriage, and life circumstances. You have to decide how best to utilize these guidelines in your own unique circumstances. Our bias, theoretically, clinically, and personally, is pro-marriage. Yet marriages that began with great promise become marginal or worse. Americans neglect their marriages, taking them for granted until the marriage enters a crisis and then attend to it. They don't want to lose the security of the marriage. People believe divorce would solve all problems, but divorces cause their own problems for self-esteem and the family. Our recommendation is to make a good faith effort to revitalize the marital bond. One person cannot save a marriage; both people need to be committed to improvement. A marriage cannot rest on one spouse sacrificing self-esteem. The revitalized marital bond would ideally reinforce each spouse's self-esteem. At a minimum, the marriage cannot undercut a spouse's self-esteem.

It is axiomatic that the best treatment is prevention. People who realize that personal and marital changes will and should happen are in a better position to manage their lives and marriage. Self-esteem and the marital bond profit from continued attention and psychological energy. Integrating individual and couple changes makes for a balanced, successful, and stable life. Creating and maintaining an intimate, stable marriage adds to life satisfaction. Good luck in utilizing these guidelines to establish and maintain a positive reciprocal relationship between self-esteem and the marital bond.

APPENDIX I

Choosing a Therapist

As we stated at the beginning, this was not meant to be a do-it-yourself therapy book. People are reluctant to consult a professional therapist, feeling that to do so is a sign of "craziness," or inadequacy, or that their marriage is in dire straits. We believe seeking professional help is a sign of psychological strength. Entering individual or marital therapy means you realize there is a problem and you've made a commitment to individual and marital growth.

The mental health field is confusing. Individual psychotherapy and marital therapy are offered by several groups of professionals including psychologists, social workers, marriage therapists, psychiatrists, sex therapists, and pastoral counselors. The background of the practitioner is of less importance than her competency in dealing with your specific problem.

Many people have health insurance that provides coverage for mental health and thus they can afford the services of a private practitioner. Those who do not have either the financial resources or insurance could consider a city or county mental health clinic, a university or medical-school mental health outpatient clinic, or a family services center. Clinics usually have a sliding fee scale—that is, the fee is based on your ability to pay.

In choosing a therapist be assertive in asking about credentials and areas of expertise as well as fees. Ask the clinician how long the therapy can be expected to last and whether there is a focus on communication, problem-solving, family of origin, or present marriage and family of creation. Ask how many of his couples stay together and how many divorce. A competent therapist will be open to discussing these issues. Be especially diligent in questioning credentials, such as university degrees and licensing, of people who call themselves personal counselors, marriage counselors, or sex counselors, since there are poorly qualified persons—and some outright quacks—in any field.

One of the best resources for obtaining a referral is to call a local professional organization such as a psychological association, marriage and family therapy association, mental health association, or mental health clinic. You can ask for a referral from a family physician, minister, or friend who has information on a therapist's areas of competence.

If you have a problem that principally concerns marriage or family issues, you could write the American Association for Marriage and Family Therapy, 1717 K Street, N.W., Room 407, Washington, D.C. 20006, for a list of certified marriage and family therapists in your area. If you are experiencing a sexual problem, you can write the American Association of Sex Educators, Counselors, and Therapists, Suite 1717, 435 N. Michigan Avenue, Chicago, IL 60611, for a list of certified sex therapists in your area.

Feel free to talk with two or three therapists before deciding on one with whom to work. Be aware of how comfortable you feel with the therapist, the degree of rapport, and whether the therapist's assessment of the problem and approach to treatment make sense to you. Once you begin therapy, give it a chance to be helpful. There are few miracle cures. Change requires commitment and is a gradual and often difficult process. Although people can benefit from short-term therapy (fewer than ten sessions), most people find the therapeutic process will take at least six months to a year. The role of the therapist is that of a consultant rather than decision-maker. Therapy requires effort, both in the session and at home. Therapy helps change attitudes, feelings, and behavior, which improves self-esteem and strengthens the marital bond.

APPENDIX II

Books for Further Reading

Alberti, Robert, and Michael Emmons. *Your Perfect Right: A Guide to Assertive Living* (Sixth Edition). San Luis Obispo, California: Impact Publishers, 1990.

Beck, Aaron. *Love Is Never Enough*. New York: Harper and Row, 1988.

Bing, Elizabeth, and Libby Coleman. *Making Love During Pregnancy*. New York: Bantam Books, 1983.

Blumstein, Philip, and Pepper Schwartz. *American Couples*. New York: William Morrow, 1983.

Boston Women's Health Book Collective. *The New Our Bodies, Ourselves*. New York: Simon and Schuster, 1984.

Butler, Robert, and Myrna Lewis. *Love and Sex After Forty*. New York: Harper and Row, 1986.

Gordon, Sol. *Why Love Is Not Enough*. Boston: Bob Adams, 1990.

Gottman, John, Cliff Notarius, Jonnie Gonso, and Howard Markman. *A Couple's Guide to Communication*. Champaign, Illinois: Research Press, 1976.

Lehner, Harriet. *The Dance of Anger*. New York: Harper and Row, 1985.

———. *The Dance of Intimacy*. New York: Harper and Row, 1989.

McCarthy, Barry. *Male Sexual Awareness*. New York: Carroll and Graf, 1988.

McCarthy, Barry, and Emily McCarthy. *Sexual Awareness*. New York: Carroll and Graf, 1984.

———. *Female Sexual Awareness*. New York: Carroll and Graf, 1989.

———. *Couple Sexual Awareness*. New York: Carroll and Graf, 1990.

Patterson, Gerald. *Families*. Champaign, Illinois: Research Press, 1981.

Tavris, Carol. *Anger: The Misunderstood Emotion*. New York: Touchstone Books, 1989.

Trafford, Abigail. *Crazy Time: Surviving Divorce*. New York: Bantam Books, 1982.